Opening the Door to Certainty

Pleasant words
profound meaning
grand philosophy:
do not exhaust your body or your mind
trying to obtain such dharma.
Trust the teachings you have received
according to your capacities
and practice them.
They will benefit your mind.

BOKAR RINPOCHE

Also by Bokar Rinpoche from ClearPoint Press
Chenrezig, Lord of Love
Meditation Advice to Beginners
Death and the Art of Dying in Tibetan Buddhism
Profound Wisdom of the Heart Sutra and Other Teachings

Opening The Door to Certainty

A Simple Arrangement of Verses Summarizing Mahamudra—The Ocean of Certainty

Bokar Rinpoche

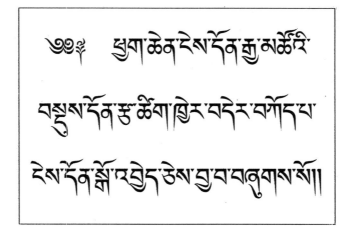

༄༅། ཕྱག་ཆེན་ངེས་དོན་རྒྱ་མཚོའི་

བསྡུས་དོན་རྩ་ཚིག་ཁྲིར་བདེར་བཀོད་པ

ངེས་དོན་སྒོ་འབྱེད་ཅེས་བྱ་བ་བཞུགས་སོ།།

Translation from French into English
Christiane Buchet

ClearPoint Press
San Francisco, California

Opening the Door to Certainty

Published by:
ClearPoint Press
PO Box 170658
San Francisco, CA 94117

The original text of this book was published in French and was titled La porte du sens definitif.

Printed in the United States of America
The paper used in this publication meets the minimum requirements of American National Standard for Information Sciences—Permanence of Paper for Printed Library Materials, ANSI Z39.48-1984
Library of Congress Catalog Card Number: 96-96789

Foreword

Bokar Rinpoche was born in Western Tibet in 1940. Considered by his peers as one of the greatest meditation masters of our times, he has written a brief text for his disciples which we are presenting here as *Opening the Door to Certainty*.

Short and compact, *Opening the Door to Certainty* is a condensed version of the Ninth Karmapa's work titled, *The Ocean of Certainty*.

The Karmapas are as well known in Tibet as the Dalai Lamas. They have headed the Tibetan Buddhist Karma Kagyu lineage of reincarnate masters since the 12th century and are the direct successors of Tilopa, Naropa, Marpa, and Milarepa.

The Ninth Karmapa, Wangchuk Dorje (1556-1603) wrote several works on meditation, the most complete and renowned being *The Ocean of Certainty (Ngedon Gyamtso)*. This voluminous book, of which to date there is no translation into any Western language, is a major classic of the Kagyupa School. It is generally used by the lamas to teach meditation.

The term *certainty* (or absolute truth, absolute meaning, definitive meaning, true meaning), used in the title of the above mentioned texts designates direct understanding through experience of the absolute nature of the mind beyond the psyche and its fluctuations, beyond concepts and emotions, beyond birth and death, and beyond space and time. The term is also used in a parallel way with the "pedagogic meaning" (or pedagogic truth) which refers to the methods used in the psychological or conceptual domains to aid in the understanding of certainty. Certainty is thus linked with absolute truth and wisdom, whereas the pedagogic meaning is associated with relative truth and skillful means.

Certainty is furthermore an equivalent term for Mahamudra, a Sanskrit word signifying "great seal" or "great symbol." Bokar Rinpoche introduces Mahamudra in the following way:

The subject of our study is Mahamudra. Mahamudra is also the mind. We call the mind that which knows, feels, and produces suffering, happiness, thoughts, sensations, feelings, and so on. We will study this mind and work upon it.

Do not think of Mahamudra as another reality, like something on a higher plane than ourselves. Mahamudra is not in the sky while we are on earth. Mahamudra is not elsewhere. We are never separated from Mahamudra, although we do not recognize it.

The purpose of Mahamudra is not to bring us something new but to introduce us to that which we already have. Mahamudra meditation allows us to internally grow accustomed to what we have discovered within ourselves through practice following the instructions we have received; it enables us to continuously dwell within this awareness.

The Tibetan word Chagya Chenpo, meaning Mahamudra, is defined as "the nature of the mind, clear light, and emptiness comprising all phenomena of samsara and nirvana."

Bokar Rinpoche's text is so concise that its reading by a beginner risks leaving the reader with a feeling of confusion. In fact, *Opening The Door to*

Certainty is not intended to develop and clarify the meditation and approach to Mahamudra; rather it serves as a reminder for those who are already engaged on the path. Written in verses, the text is easy to memorize and recite ritually. Bokar Rinpoche composed this work at the request of students. It is intended to help students easily recall the various aspects of the path, showing them the exact place of each point, and inviting them to progress and deepen their understanding.

The French and English translations were made at the request and with the help of Bokar Rinpoche. They are mainly intended for the disciples who attend the meditation seminars that Bokar Rinpoche conducts regularly in India. These translations will also be of some interest to those who are engaged on the profound paths of Buddhism and study the Tibetan language.

We have tried to remain as close as possible to the Tibetan text. As far as possible, we have selected literal terms for the translation of technical terms, avoiding their interpretation.

In spite of all efforts, there may be some mistakes in our translations. May those who detect any errors be thanked in advance for sending us their comments.

—Choky Singe (François Jacquemart)

Publisher's Acknowledgement

The publisher gratefully acknowledges the generous support of people who help in the different phases of the production. Thanks to Lama Chodrak, Tony Albino, Ngodup T. Burkhar, Eva Davidson, Jason Espada, Rosemary Gilpin, Karen Graham, Juanita Hall, Wendy Péclet-Harlow, Elson Snow, and Isao Tanaka.

Translator's Note

At the request of Bokar Rinpoche, I translated *Opening the Door to Certainty* from French into English. Although many people with more expertise than I, have assisted in this project, I, alone, am responsible for any errors. It is my sincere wish that despite its imperfection, this translation will carry the original meaning and make accessible these profound teachings to those who want to study and practice them. May the excellent activity of Bokar Rinpoche benefit all beings.

—*Christiane Buchet*

༄༅། ཕྱག་ཆེན་ངེས་དོན་རྒྱ་མཚོའི་བསྡུས་དོན་རྩ་ཚིག་ཁྲིར་བདེར་བཀོད་པ
ངེས་དོན་སྒྲོ་འབྱེད་ཅེས་བྱ་བ་བཞུགས་སོ།།

Table of Contents

Opening The Door to Certainty

A Simple Arrangement of Verses Summarizing Mahamudra—The Ocean of Certainty

PRELIMINARIES

༄༅། ཨོཾ་སྭ་སྟི། །བླ་མ་ལྷ་དང་རང་སེམས་རྣམས། །དབྱེར་མེད་གཉུག་མའི་ངང་དུ་གཅིག
།དེ་ལ་བདག་ནི་དུས་ཀུན་ཏུ། །ཕྱག་འཚལ་སྐྱབས་སུ་ཉེ་བར་མཆི། དེ་ལ་འདིར་གང་དག་ཕྱག་རྒྱ་ཆེན་
པོ་ལྷན་ཅིག་སྐྱེས་སྦྱོར་གྱི་ཁྲིད་ངེས་དོན་རྒྱ་མཚོ་ལ་འཇུག་པར་འདོད་པ་དེ་དག་ལ་ཕན་པའི་བློས་གཞུང་གི་ས་བཅད་རྣམས་
ཟུར་དུ་བསྒྲིལ་ཅིང་དེ་དང་དེའི་ཐད་ཀྱི་སྒོམ་རིམ་རྣམས་གཟུང་བདེ་བའི་ཕྱིར་བསྡུས་དོན་རྩ་ཚིག་ལྟ་བུ་འམ་འདོན་སྒོམ་སྦྲག་
མར་བྱས་ཀྱང་རུང་བའི་ཉུང་གསལ་ཞིག་སྤེལ་བར་བྱའོ། དེ་ལ་སྔོན་འགྲོ་དང་། དངོས་གཞི། རྗེས་གསུམ་ལས། དང་པོ་སྔོན་
འགྲོ་ལ། ཐུན་མོང་གི་སྔོན་འགྲོ་དང་། ཐུན་མོང་མ་ཡིན་པའི་སྔོན་འགྲོ ཁྱད་པར་གྱི་སྔོན་འགྲོ་དང་གསུམ་ལས། དང་པོ་ཐུན་
མོང་གི་སྔོན་འགྲོ་ལ་བཞི་སྟེ། དལ་འབྱོར་རྙེད་དཀའ། འཆི་བ་མི་རྟག་པ། ལས་རྒྱུ་འབྲས། འཁོར་བའི་ཉེས་དམིགས་སྒོམ་
པའོ། དང་པོ་ནི། ན་མོ་གུ་རུ་བྷྱཿ །གང་ཞིག་དམ་ཆོས་ཚུལ་བཞིན་སྒྲུབ་པ་ལ། །རྣམ་གཡེང་སྤོང་
སྟེ་ཐོག་མར་བསྒོམ་བྱ་ནི། །དལ་བརྒྱད་འབྱོར་པ་བཅུ་ལྡན་རྟེན་བཟང་འདི། །རྙེད་པར་དཀའ་
ཞིང་ཕན་ཐོགས་ཆེས་ཆེ་བས། །ཡིད་བཞིན་ནོར་བུ་དང་ནི་ཆོས་མཚུངས་ཤིང་། །ཁྱད་པར་རྡོ་རྗེ་
ཐེག་པ་ལ་བརྟེན་ནས། །ཚེ་གཅིག་བྱང་ཆུབ་སྒྲུབ་ལ་ཁམས་དྲུག་ལྡན། །རྡོ་རྗེའི་ལུས་འདི་དེ་
བས་ཀྱང་ནི་དཀོན། །དེ་ཡང་རྒྱུ་དང་དཔེ་དང་གྲངས་གསུམ་གྱིས། །རྙེད་པར་དཀའ་ཞིང་རྙེད་
ཀྱང་ཆེས་ཤིན་ཏུ། །འཇིག་པར་སླ་བས་ད་རེས་ནས་བཟུང་སྟེ། དམ་ཆོས་ག་ཤའ་ར་མ་སྒྲུབ་ལ་
འབད་པར་བྱ། གཉིས་པ་ནི། །ཕྱི་ནང་སྣོད་བཅུད་འདུས་བྱས་ཆོས་ཐམས་ཅད། །མཐའ་བཞིའི་
ཚུལ་གྱིས་སྐད་ཅིག་ཀྱང་མི་རྟག །ཁྱད་པར་འགྲོ་བའི་ཚེ་སྲོག་ལྟུང་གསེབ་ཀྱི། །མར་མེ་དང་ནི་
ཆུ་ཡི་ཆུ་བུར་བཞིན། །དེ་ཡང་བདག་ཉིད་ངེས་པར་འཆི་བ་དང་། །ནམ་འཆི་ཆ་མེད་པར་ནི་
མྱུར་དུ་འཆི། །འཆི་རྐྱེན་མང་ཞིང་མི་འདོད་བཞིན་དུ་འཆི། །དེ་ལ་གང་གིས་ཀྱང་ནི་བཟློག་མི་
ནུས། །འཆི་ཚེ་སྡུག་བསྔལ་བཟོད་གླག་མེད་མྱོང་ཞིང་། །དེ་ཚེ་དམ་པའི་ཆོས་ལས་སྐྱབས་
གཞན་མེད། །དེས་ན་བློ་སྣ་བསྐྲངས་ཤིང་སྐྱོ་ཤས་བསྐྱེད། །ཡོང་མེད་བསམ་པ་དྲག་པོས་དགེ

Text

Om Soti. The lama, deities, and my own mind are inseparable in the natural state. At all times, prostrating, I place myself completely under their protection.

With the mind of benefitting those who wish to follow the guide for integrating the "coemergent Mahamudra" that is The Ocean of Certainty, *I have outlined the structure of the text. I have composed a short version epitomizing the meaning, which may be used as summary verses easing the approach of meditation stages or for combining recitation and meditation. It is divided into three parts: preliminaries, body of the practice, and post practice.*

Preliminaries

I. Common Preliminaries

1. Freedoms & Richnesses of the Human Existence so Difficult to Obtain

Namo Guru Bay. Those who wish to practice the holy Dharma correctly must abandon distractions and first reflect upon this excellent support, endowed with the eight freedoms and the ten richnesses. So difficult to obtain and extremely beneficial, this support is comparable to a wish-fulfilling jewel. Even more rare is the vajra-body with the six elements, by which it is possible to accomplish Awakening in a single lifetime through the practice of the Vajrayana. The difficulty in obtaining human existence is explained by causes, comparisons, and numbers. Even if we have obtained it, it is easily destroyed. This is why, from now on, we must devote all our efforts only to the practice of the Dharma.

2. Death and Impermanence

All compound outer and inner phenomena, container and beings are not permanent even for the slightest instant, as is shown by the four ends. Particularly, the life of beings is like a flame exposed to the wind or like a bubble on the surface of the water. It is certain that I will die. Although the moment of death is uncertain, I will die very soon. The causes of death are many and even if I do not want it, I will die. No one has the power to ward off death. At the time of death, intolerable suffering is experienced. There is no other refuge but the holy Dharma. Consequently, without wasting time, we generate disenchantment. We feel a sense of urgency and ardently give ourselves up to virtue.

ལ་འབྱུངས། གསུམ་པ་ནི། འཆི་རྗེས་སྣུམ་ཟད་མར་མེ་ལྟ་བུའམ། །ཡང་ན་གར་སྐྱེ་རང་དབང་ཡོད་མིན་ཏེ། །དབང་མེད་ལས་ཀྱི་རྗེས་སུ་ངེས་པར་འབྱུངས། །ཕྱིར་ན་བདེ་སྡུག་སྣང་བ་སྣ་ཚོགས་པ། །དགེ་སྡིག་ལས་ཀྱི་འབྲས་བུ་ཡིན་པར་གསུངས། །དེ་ཡང་དགེ་བཅུ་སྤྱད་ལས་བདེ་འགྲོ་དང་། ཉོན་མོངས་དབང་གིས་མི་དགེ་བཅུ་སྤྱད་པས། །ངན་འགྲོར་སྐྱེ་བའི་ཚུལ་སོགས་ཞིབ་ཏུ་བསམ། །མདོར་ན་རང་གིས་བྱས་པའི་རྣམ་སྨིན་ནི། །ཆུད་དུ་མི་ཟ་ནམ་ཞིག་རང་ཉིད་ཀྱིས། །མྱོང་བར་ངེས་པས་དགེ་སྡིག་བླང་དོར་ཀུན། །ཚུལ་བཞིན་འབད་ལ་རང་རྒྱུད་གཞིག་འབྲེལ་བྱོས། བཞི་པ་ནི། །ཁམས་གསུམ་འཁོར་བ་རིགས་དྲུག་གར་སྐྱེས་ཀྱང་། །སྡུག་བསྔལ་གསུམ་གྱིས་རྟག་ཏུ་རབ་མནར་ཏེ། །དེ་ཡང་ཤིན་ཏུ་དོས་དྲག་ཡུན་རིང་པོར། །དམྱལ་བ་ཚ་གྲང་ཡི་དྭགས་བཀྲེས་སྐོམ་དང་། །དུད་འགྲོ་གཅིག་ལ་གཅིག་ཟའི་སྡུག་བསྔལ་དང་། །མི་ལ་སྐྱེ་རྒ་ན་འཆི་སོགས་དེ་བཞིན། །ལྷ་མིན་འཐབ་རྩོད་ལྷ་ལ་འཕོ་ལྟུང་གི །སྡུག་བསྔལ་དེ་རྣམས་མྱོང་བའི་ཚུལ་བསམ་སྟེ། །ལྟར་སྣང་སྲིད་པའི་བདེ་འབྱོར་ཕྲ་མོ་འདི། །དུག་དང་སྦྲུར་བའི་ཟས་བཞིན་རིང་དུ་དོར། །འཁོར་བ་མེ་འོབས་དང་འདྲ་འདི་ལས་ནི། །ངེས་པར་ཐར་བའི་ཐབས་ཤིག་ད་རེས་རེམ། གཉིས་པ་ཐུན་མོང་མ་ཡིན་པའི་སྔོན་འགྲོ་བཞི་སྦྱོར་ནི། རྒྱུད་སྔོན་དུ་རུང་བའམ་ཅི་བྱས་ཐར་པའི་ལམ་དུ་འགྲོ་བ་སྐྱབས་འགྲོ་སེམས་བསྐྱེད་ཀྱི་ཁྲིད་དང་། སྡིག་སྒྲིབ་དག་པར་བྱེད་པ་རྡོ་རྗེ་སེམས་དཔའི་སྒོམ་བཟླས། ཚོགས་གཉིས་རྫོགས་པར་བྱེད་པ་མཎྜལ། བྱིན་རླབས་མྱུར་དུ་འཇུག་པར་བྱེད་པ་བླ་མའི་རྣལ་འབྱོར་གྱི་ཁྲིད་དོ། དང་པོ་ནི། །དེ་ལྟར་སྲིད་པའི་སྡུག་བསྔལ་ལས་སྐྱོབ་པའི། །སྐྱབས་ནི་དཀོན་མཆོག་གསུམ་ལས་གཞན་མ་མཆིས། །དེས་ན་བདག་གཞན་མཁའ་ཁྱབ་འགྲོ་བ་ཀུན། སྐྱབས་སུ་འགྲོ་ལ་འདི་ལྟར་གསལ་གདབ་སྟེ། །མདུན་མཁར་དཔག་བསམ་ལྗོན་ཤིང་ཡལ་ག་ལྔ། །གྱེས་པའི་དབུས་མར་སེང་ཁྲི་པད་ཟླའི་སྟེང་། །རྩ་བའི་བླ་མ་རྡོ་རྗེ་འཆང་དབང་ནི། །མཚན་དཔེས་རབ་རྫོགས་ལྷམ

3. Action, Cause, and Effect [Karma]

Once dead, we are like a lamp whose oil is exhausted. Wherever we are reborn, we cannot do it freely, but it is certain that we are led by karma and have no control of our own. It is commonly said that the various manifestations of happiness and suffering are the result of positive or negative acts. Accomplishing the ten positive acts leads to birth in fortunate realms while accomplishing the ten negative acts under the influence of conflicting emotions brings birth in unfortunate realms. We reflect thoroughly on this process. Briefly, the result of the ripening karma of our actions, without vanishing, will definitively be experienced by us alone. Therefore, we should meticulously examine the stream of our mind to correctly apply perfect discrimination between positive and negative acts.

4. Defective Nature of Samsara

Wherever we are born within the six cyclic realms of the three spheres, we are continuously tormented by the three types of suffering. There are the atrocious and long sufferings of the beings of hot and cold hells; hungry ghosts endure hunger and thirst, and animals devour each other. Human beings undergo the suffering of birth, old age, sickness, death, and much other suffering. Demi-gods suffer from quarreling, and gods from transmigration and downfall. We reflect on the ways these sufferings are experienced, in order to reject the insignificant pleasures and possessions of the world of becoming as food mixed with poison. Samsara is like a raging fire. We are determined from this moment on to apply a method that is certain to free ourselves from samsara.

II. Specific Preliminaries

Within the four specific preliminaries, we find:

- *instructions for taking Refuge and generating the mind of Awakening which transform the mind into an adequate vessel and bring all acts onto the path of liberation*
- *Vajrasattva meditation with recitation of the mantra, which purifies negative acts and veils*
- *mandala practice which perfects the two accumulations*
- *instruction on guru yoga which quickly confers grace*

1. Taking Refuge and Generating the Mind of Awakening

We should not search for any refuge other than the Three Jewels to protect us from the suffering of samsara. While we take refuge together with all the beings of the universe, we do the following visualization.

མི་ལྡན་ནེར་བཞུགས། །དེ་སྟེང་བརྒྱུད་པའི་བླ་མ་ཐོ་བརྩེགས་དང་། །མདུན་གཡས་རྒྱབ་དང་
གཡོན་དུ་རིམ་པ་བཞིན། །ཡི་དམ་སངས་རྒྱས་ཆོས་དང་དགེ་འདུན་རྣམས། །སྤྲིན་གྱི་ཕུང་པོ་
གཏིབས་བཞིན་བཞུགས་པ་ལ། །བདག་སོགས་འགྲོ་ཀུན་རྫོགས་བྱང་མ་ཐོབ་བར། །སྐྱབས་
སུ་འགྲོ་ཞིང་བྱང་ཆུབ་སེམས་མཆོག་བསྐྱེད། །མཐའ་མར་སྐྱབས་ཡུལ་འོད་ཞུ་བདག་ཉིད་ཀྱི།
།སྒོ་གསུམ་ལ་ཐིམ་གཅིག་མའི་རང་ངོར་ཞོག གཉིས་པ་ནི། །ཐོག་མེད་ནས་བསགས་སྡིག་ལྟུང་
ཅི་མཆིས་ཀུན། །སྟོབས་བཞིའི་སྒོ་ནས་བཤགས་ཤིང་ཁྱད་པར་དུ། །གཉེན་པོ་ཀུན་ཏུ་སྤྱོད་
པའི་སྟོབས་ཀྱི་མཆོག །རྡོ་རྗེ་སེམས་དཔའི་སྒོམ་བཟླས་ལ་འཇུག་ན། །རང་ཉིད་ཐ་མལ་གནས་
པའི་སྤྱི་གཙུག་ཏུ། །བླ་མ་རྡོ་རྗེ་སེམས་དཔའ་སྐུ་མདོག་དཀར། །ཕྱག་གཡས་རྡོ་རྗེ་རྩེ་ལྔ་
ཐུགས་ཀར་འཛིན། །གཡོན་པས་དྲིལ་བུ་དཀུར་རྟེན་སེམས་སྐྱིལ་བཞུགས། །སྣང་ལ་རང་
བཞིན་མེད་པའི་སྐུར་གསལ་བའི། །ཐུགས་ཀར་ཟླ་སྟེང་ཧཱུྃ་ལ་ཡིག་བརྒྱས་བསྐོར། །དེ་ལས་
བདུད་རྩིའི་རྒྱུན་བབས་ཚངས་བུག་ནས། །ཞུགས་ཏེ་སྡིག་སྒྲིབ་ཉམས་ཆག་མ་ལུས་སྦྱངས།
།སླར་ཡང་གསོལ་བ་བཏབ་པས་དགྱེས་བཞིན་དུ། །ཁྱོད་ཀྱི་སྡིག་སྒྲིབ་ཐམས་ཅད་དག་གོ་ཞེས།
།གསུང་གིས་དབུགས་དབྱུང་དང་བཅས་འོད་དུ་ཞུ། །རང་ཐིམ་རྡོ་རྗེ་གསུམ་དང་དབྱེར་མེད་
གྱུར། གསུམ་པ་ནི། །ཞིང་ཁམས་འབུལ་བའི་ཐབས་མཆོག་ལ་བརྟེན་ནས། །བསོད་ནམས་ཡེ་
ཤེས་ཚོགས་གཉིས་གསོག་པར་བྱ། །དེ་ལ་སྨྲོན་གྱི་དྲི་མས་མ་གོས་པའི། །རིན་ཆེན་ལས་གྲུབ་
སྒྲུབ་པའི་མཎྜལ་ཉིད། །མཚན་ཉིད་ཡོངས་རྫོགས་གཞལ་ཡས་ཁང་གསལ་བའི། །དབུས་སུ་
རྩ་བརྒྱུད་བླ་མ་ཕྱོགས་བཞིར། །ཡི་དམ་སངས་རྒྱས་ཆོས་དང་དགེ་འདུན་དང་། །དཔའ་བོ་
མཁའ་འགྲོ་ཡེ་ཤེས་སྲུང་མར་བཅས། །ལེགས་པར་གསལ་བཏབ་རང་ཉིད་དེའི་མདུན་དུ།
མཆོད་པའི་མཎྜལ་ཐོགས་ཏེ་རི་རབ་དང་། །གླིང་བཞི་གླིང་ཕྲན་ལ་སོགས་བྱེ་བ་བརྒྱ། །གཞན་

Facing us in space, the noble wish-fulfilling tree is divided into five branches. At the center where the branches converge, on a lion throne, a lotus, and the moon, sits the root lama, the sovereign Vajradhara. He is radiant and brilliant, perfectly endowed with all the physical marks and signs. Above him, the lamas of the lineage are placed one above the other. Then, in the front, on the right, rear, and left, respectively, are the yidams, the Buddhas, the Dharma, and the Sangha, gathered like clusters of clouds. Until perfect Awakening is attained, we take refuge and generate the sublime mind of Awakening, together with all beings. Finally, the sources of refuge dissolve into light and melt through our three gates. We dwell in the essence of the natural state.

2. Vajrasattva Meditation with Recitation of the Mantra

Whatever negative acts and transgression of vows we have accumulated since time without beginning, they are neutralized by the four strengths. The Vajrasattva meditation with the recitation of the mantra has the sublime power of acting like a complete antidote. Remaining in ordinary form, we imagine that above our head there is the lama Vajrasattva, white in color, holding in his right hand at the level of the heart a five-pronged vajra, and in his left hand placed at his hip, a bell; he sits in the Bodhisattva posture. We visualize his transparent body as appearing, yet lacking substantiality. In his heart, on a moon disc, the one hundred syllables are circling the syllable HUNG. From there, nectar pours down and enters us through the Brahma orifice. The nectar purifies faults and veils, damages and violation of the vows without exception. Then, we again address a prayer to Vajrasattva and rejoicing, he replies, "You are purified of all faults and veils." Thus we are rejuvenated. Vajrasattva then dissolves into light and melts into us. We become one with his three vajras.

3. Offering the Mandala

Through the sublime method of offering the universe, the two accumulations of merit and wisdom are accomplished. To do so, we need an accomplishment mandala made of precious unstained material. We visualize it perfectly in front of us as a magnificent palace endowed with all characteristics. At its center, there are the root lamas and the lamas of the lineage; in the four directions, there are the yidams, the Buddhas, the Dharma, the Sangha, and the dakas, dakinis, and wisdom protectors. Holding the offering mandala, we offer, through making them appear in our mind, myriads of Mount Meru, continents and subcontinents, our body, possessions, positive accumulation, all that belongs to us and to the beings of the universe without exception. Through the power of this offering, the two accumulations are accomplished. The deities rejoice, dissolve into light and melt into us. We become indivisible.

ཡང་བདག་སོགས་མཁའ་མཉམ་འགྲོ་ཀུན་གྱི། །ལུས་དང་ལོངས་སྤྱོད་དགེ་ཚོགས་ཅི་མཆིས་ཀུན། །མ་ལུས་བློ་ཡིས་བླངས་ཏེ་ཕུལ་བའི་མཐུས། །ཚོགས་གཉིས་རབ་རྫོགས་ལྷ་རྣམས་དགྱེས་པའི་ངང་། །འོད་ཞུ་རང་ལ་ཐིམ་པས་གཉིས་མེད་གྱུར། བཞི་པ་ནི། ཡོན་ཏན་ཀུན་གྱི་གཞིར་གྱུར་ཁྱད་པར་དུ། །དོན་དམ་ཕྱག་ཆེན་རྟོགས་པའི་ཐབས་མཆོག་ནི། །དཔལ་ལྡན་བླ་མའི་བྱིན་རླབས་ལས་གཞན་མེད། །དེ་ཕྱིར་དེ་ཡི་རྣལ་འབྱོར་བྱ་བ་ལ། །རང་ཉིད་ཡི་དམ་ལྷར་གསལ་སྤྱི་གཙུག་ཏུ། །རྩ་བའི་བླ་མ་རྡོ་རྗེ་འཆང་དབང་པོ། །དེ་སྟེང་བརྒྱུད་པའི་བླ་མ་རྣམས་ཐོ་བརྩེགས། །གཞན་ཡང་ཡི་དམ་སངས་རྒྱས་བྱང་སེམས་དང་། །དཔའ་བོ་མཁའ་འགྲོ་ཡི་ཤེས་སྲུང་མས་བསྐོར། །དེ་ལ་མཆོད་ཅིང་གདུང་བས་གསོལ་བཏབ་མཐུས། །འཁོར་རྣམས་གཙོར་ཐིམ་གཙོ་བོ་དེ་ཉིད་ནི། །སྐྱབས་གནས་ཀུན་འདུས་ཉིད་གྱུར་སླར་ཡང་དེར། །དབང་བསྐུར་གསོལ་བ་བཏབ་པས་དབང་བཞི་ཐོབ། །སྒྲིབ་བཞི་དག་ཅིང་སྐུ་བཞིའི་ས་བོན་བཞག །དེ་ནས་བླ་མ་དགྱེས་བཞིན་འོད་དུ་ཞུ། །རང་ཐིམ་ཕྱག་ཆེན་ངང་དུ་མཉམ་པར་བཞག གསུམ་པ་ཁྱད་པར་གྱི་སྔོན་འགྲོ་བཞི་ནི། རྒྱུའི་རྐྱེན་དང་། བདག་པོའི་རྐྱེན། དམིགས་པའི་རྐྱེན། དེ་མ་ཐག་པའི་རྐྱེན་དང་བཞི་ལས། དང་པོ་ནི། །རང་རྒྱུད་ལེགས་པར་དུལ་ཅིང་ངེས་འབྱུང་དང་། །ཐར་འདོད་བསམ་པས་ཞེན་ཁྲིས་ཀུན་བཅད་དེ། །ཤིན་ཏུ་དབེན་པའི་གནས་སུ་ཕྱི་ནང་གི །རྣམ་གཡེང་མེད་པར་བྱ་བཏང་ཁོ་ནར་གནས། གཉིས་པ་ནི། ཕྱག་རྒྱ་ཆེན་པོ་རྟོགས་པར་བྱེད་པའི་ལམ་བླ་མ་ཁོ་ན་ལ་རག་ལས་པས། ཡང་དག་པའི་དགེ་བའི་བཤེས་གཉེན་གྱིས་ཟིན་པ་ཞིག་དགོས་ཤིང་། དེ་ལའང་གང་ཟག་བརྒྱུད་པའི་བླ་མ། བདེ་གཤེགས་བཀའི་བླ་མ། སྣང་བ་བརྡའི་བླ་མ། དོན་དམ་ཆོས་ཉིད་ཀྱི་བླ་མ་དང་བཞི་ལས། དང་པོ་ནི། །རྡོ་རྗེ་འཆང་ནས་རྩ་བའི་བླ་མའི་བར། །བྱིན་རླབས་དང་ནི་མན་ངག་ལ་སོགས་པའི། །རྒྱུན་རྣམས་མ་ཆད་རིམ་པར་གཅིག་ནས་གཅིག །ཡང་དག་བརྒྱུད་དེ་བྱོན་པའི་བླ་མའོ། གཉིས་པ་ནི། །བླ་མས་བསྟན་པ་ཇི་

4. Guru Yoga

The basis of all qualities, particularly the sublime method of realizing ultimate truth—Mahamudra—is nothing other than the grace of the glorious lama. Therefore, to accomplish this yoga, we visualize ourselves as a yidam. Above our head, there is the root lama, the sovereign Vajradhara. Above him, there are the lamas of the lineage arranged in tiers. Vajradhara is also surrounded by the yidams, Buddhas, Bodhisattvas, dakas, dakinis, and wisdom protectors. We make offerings and pray to them with fervor. By the power of this, the retinue melts into the main figure, and the latter becomes the union of all the sources of refuge. We pray for Vajradhara to confer the empowerments, and we receive the four empowerments. We are purified from the four veils while receiving the seed of the four Bodies. Then the lama rejoices, melts into light, and is absorbed into us. We dwell evenly in the state of Mahamudra.

III. Special Preliminaries

1. Causal Factor

Perfectly mastering our stream of mind, having cut away any attachment and bond, inclined to disinterest for this world, and inclined to the wish for liberation, we dwell alone in a very secluded place and renounce any activity containing outer or inner distractions.

2. Principal Factor

Because the path that brings us to realize Mahamudra depends solely on the lama, we need to be directed by an authentic spiritual friend. This master assumes four aspects.

a) The master as human being belonging to a lineage

That is a lama belonging to a perfectly pure lineage through which the continuity of grace, direct instructions, and so on, have been transmitted without interruption from Vajradhara to our root lama.

b) The master as Awakened word

When the certainty inspired by the lama's teaching is obtained in our mind, and when we experience that this teaching is in no way contradictory to the word of the Buddha, all the teachings of the Buddha manifest as direct instructions.

བཞིན་རང་སེམས་ལ། །ངེས་པ་སྐྱེས་ཤིང་དེ་ཉིད་རྒྱལ་བའི་བཀའ། །གང་ལའང་འགལ་མེད་ཉམས་སྐྱོང་སྐྱེ་བའི་ཕྱིར། །གསུང་རབ་ཐམས་ཅད་གདམས་པར་འཆར་བས་སོ། གསུམ་པ་ནི། །འབྱུང་དང་འབྱུང་བ་ལས་གྱུར་ཕྱི་ནང་གི། །འཁོར་འདས་དངོས་པོའི་ཆོས་རྣམས་ཐམས་ཅད་ཀྱིས། །ལམ་གྱི་ཚུལ་རྣམས་བརྡ་དང་དཔེའི་སྒོ་ནས། །སྟོན་ཕྱིར་དངོས་ཀུན་བླ་མར་མ་གྱུར་མེད། བཞི་པ་ནི། དཔལ་ལྡན་བླ་མས་ཇི་ལྟར་ངོ་སྤྲོད་པའི། །རང་སེམས་གནས་ལུགས་ཕྱིན་ཅི་མ་ལོག་པར། །མངོན་སུམ་མཐོང་རྟོགས་གཏན་ལ་ཕེབས་པ་དེས། །ཆོས་རྣམས་ཀུན་གྱི་དེ་བཞིན་ཉིད་ཀྱང་རྟོགས། གསུམ་པ་དམིགས་རྐྱེན་ནི། །ཕྱི་ནང་གྲུབ་མཐའི་བློ་ཡིས་མ་བསྒྱུར་ཅིང་། །རྟོག་པས་མ་བསླད་གདོད་མའི་གནས་ལུགས་ཀྱི། །སེམས་ཀྱི་ངོ་བོ་སྐུ་གསུམ་གྱི་རོལ་པ། །དེ་ཉིད་ཁོ་ན་ཉམས་སུ་བླང་བྱའོ། བཞི་པ་དེ་མ་ཐག་རྐྱེན་ནི། །དངོས་གཞི་ཉམས་སུ་ལེན་པའི་གནས་སྐབས་སུ། །བསྒོམ་བྱ་སྒོམ་བྱེད་རྣམ་པར་མི་རྟོག་ཅིང་། །སྣང་བླང་རེ་དོགས་བཟོ་བཅོས་མ་བྱས་པའི། །ཐ་མལ་ཤེས་པའི་ངོ་བོ་ཁོ་ནར་སྐྱོངས། །གཉིས་པ་དངོས་གཞི་ལ། ཞི་གནས་དང་། ལྷག་མཐོང་གཉིས། དང་པོ་ལ་འང་སྤྱི་དང་བྱེ་བྲག་གོ། དང་པོ་ལ་ལུས་གནད་དང་སེམས་གནད་གཉིས་ལས། དང་པོ་ནི། །ལུས་གནད་རྣམ་པར་སྣང་མཛད་ཆོས་བདུན་ཏེ། །རྐང་པ་རྡོར་སྐྱིལ་ལག་པ་མཉམ་པར་བཞག །དཔུང་པ་རྒོད་གཤོག་ལྟར་བརྒྱང་མགྲིན་པ་ནི། །ལྕགས་ཀྱུ་ལྟར་དགུག་སྐྱལ་ཚིགས་མདའ་ལྟར་བསྲང་། །མིག་ནི་སྣ་རྩེའི་སོར་བཞིའི་ནམ་མཁར་གཏད། །མཆུ་དང་སོ་ནི་རང་བབས་བཞག་ཅིང་ལྕེ། །ཡ་རྐན་ལ་སྦྱར་བདེ་བའི་སྟན་ལ་འཁོད། གཉིས་པ་ནི། །སེམས་ཀྱི་གནད་ནི་དེ་ཡང་ཇི་སྐད་དུ། །མི་མནོ་མི་བསམ་མི་སེམས་མི་སྒོམ་ཞིང་། །མི་དཔྱད་རང་སོར་བཞག་ཅེས་གསུངས་པ་བཞིན། །དགག་སྒྲུབ་སྤང་བླང་རེ་དོགས་དངོས་འཛིན་གྱི། །ཨ་འཐས་ཞེན་པ་དང་བྲལ་ཐ་མལ་གྱི། །ཤེས་པ་སྐད་ཅིག་མ་འདིའི་ངོ་བོ་རུ། །ལྷོད་ཀྱིས་གློད་ལ་མ་ཡེངས་རྩེ་གཅིག་ཏུ།

c) The master as symbolic appearances
Given that all material phenomena of samsara and nirvana, outer or inner, whether elements or transformations of elements, show us the aspects of the path by signs and by metaphors, there is nothing other than the lama.

d) The master as ultimate nature (dharmata)
Through the direct vision, the realization, and the sure and unmistaken understanding of the nature of our own mind, we realize the ultimate nature of all phenomena.

3. Objective Factor
Not entering the considerations of philosophical systems, Buddhist or non-Buddhist, and not tarnished by concepts, we practice only with the essence of the mind, as the primordial mode of being, the play of the three Bodies.

4. Immediate Factor
When we accomplish the body of the practice, without conceiving an object of meditation or a meditator, we only maintain the essence of ordinary awareness without accepting or rejecting anything, without hope or fear, and without mental fabrication.

Body of the Practice

I. Mental Calming [Shinay]

A. GENERAL PRINCIPLES

1. Basic Physical Posture
The basic physical posture comprises the seven points of Vairocana.
1) the legs in vajra posture
2) the hands in the mudra of meditation
3) the shoulders spread like the wings of a vulture
4) the neck slightly bent like a hook
5) the spine straight as an arrow
6) the eyes gazing into space about four fingers from the tip of the nose
7) the lips and teeth naturally relaxed, tongue against the palate

We position ourselves on a comfortable seat.

།གསལ་སྟོང་འཛིན་མེད་མ་བཅོས་ལྷུག་པར་ཞོག ། གཉིས་པ་བྱེ་བྲག་ལ། སེམས་མ་ཟིན་པ་ཟིན་པར་བྱེད་པ། ཟིན་པ་བརྟན་པར་བྱེད་པ། བརྟན་པ་བོགས་དབྱུང་བ་བཅས་ལས། དང་པོ་ལ། དམིགས་པ་དང་བཅས་ཏེ་སེམས་འཛིན་པ། དམིགས་པ་མེད་པར་སེམས་འཛིན་པ། རླུང་ལ་སེམས་འཛིན་པའོ། དང་པོ་ལ། ཕྱིར་འཛིན་པ་དང་ནང་དུ་འཛིན་པ་གཉིས། དང་པོ་ལ་མ་དག་པ་ལ་སེམས་འཛིན་པ་དང་། དག་པ་ལ་སེམས་འཛིན་པའོ། དང་པོ་ནི། །ལྟ་སྟངས་ལུས་གནད་ལེགས་པར་གཅས་ཏེ་འཁོད། །མདུན་གྱི་གཞི་རུ་ཀ་བ་རྩིག་པ་སོགས། །རག་པའི་གཟུགས་གང་ཞིག་ལ་གཏད་པ་ལས། །གཞན་དུ་མ་ཡེངས་རྩེ་གཅིག་མཉམ་པར་བཞག །དེ་བཞིན་མདུན་དུ་ཤིང་བུའམ་རྡེའུ་སྟེ། །ཕྲ་བའི་གཟུགས་ལ་མ་ཡེངས་སེམས་འཛིན་ཞིང་། །གཞན་ཡང་མར་མེ་ནམ་མཁའ་དེ་བཞིན་དུ། །སྨིན་མཚམས་ཐིག་ལེ་དཀར་པོ་སྲན་མ་ཙམ། །དམིགས་པའི་རྟེན་དུ་བྱས་ལ་སེམས་འཛིན་ནོ། གཉིས་པ་དག་པ་ལ་སེམས་འཛིན་པ་ནི། །མདུན་དུ་རྫོགས་པའི་སངས་རྒྱས་བཅོམ་ལྡན་འདས། །སྐུ་མདོག་ཆ་ལུགས་མཚན་དང་དཔེ་བྱད་སོགས། །ལེགས་པར་གསལ་བཏབ་དད་གུས་དང་བཅས་ཏེ། །དེ་ལ་རྩེ་གཅིག་གཏད་དེ་སེམས་གཟུང་བྱ། གཉིས་པ་ནང་དུ་སེམས་འཛིན་པ་ནི། །རང་གི་སྙིང་གར་པད་འདབ་བརྒྱད་པའི་ལྟེར། །ཡི་དམ་གང་རུང་བསྐྱེད་ནས་བླ་མ་སྒོམ། །ཡང་ན་དེ་དག་གི་ནི་ངོ་བོ་རུ། །འོད་ཀྱི་གོང་བུར་གསལ་ལ་སེམས་གཟུང་ངོ་། །དེ་ལྟར་དམིགས་རྟེན་རྣམས་ལ་མ་ཡེངས་བར། །ལྟ་སྟངས་དང་བཅས་གྲིམས་ལྷོད་སྐྱོན་དང་བྲལ། །དྲན་པའི་རྒྱུང་སོ་ཙམ་ལས་བཟོ་མེད་དང་། །སྤྱང་བླང་རེ་དོགས་མེད་པར་རང་བབས་སུ། ལྷོད་ཀྱི་གློད་ལ་འཇོལ་ལེ་ཤིག་གེར་ཞོག གཉིས་པ་དམིགས་པ་མེད་པ་ལ་སེམས་འཛིན་པ་ནི། །ཕྱི་ནང་དངོས་པོའི་ཆོས་རྣམས་ཐམས་ཅད་ཀུན། །སྟོང་ཆེན་གཅིག་ཅར་པ་ལ་སེམས་འཛིན་པའམ། །ཡང་ན་དེ་རྣམས་གཅིག་ལ་གཅིག་ཐིམ་ཞིང་། །སྟོང་ཆེན་འོད་གསལ་བ་ལ་མཉམ་པར་བཞག གསུམ་པ་རླུང་ལ་སེམས་འཛིན་པ་ནི། །རླུང་ལ་སེམས་འཛིན་པ་ནི་ལུས་ཅན་ལ།

2. Basic Mental Attitude

The basic attitude of the mind is pointed out in these terms: "Do not reflect, do not conceive, do not think, do not meditate, do not analyze, rest naturally." The spontaneous ordinary awareness is free of stopping and creating, refusal and acceptance, hope or fear, attachment and grasping to a reality. We rest in this essence, relaxed in the relaxation, without distraction, with one-pointed attention, without grasping to clarity or emptiness, in the nondoing.

B. SPECIFIC METHODS

1. Anchoring the Wandering Mind

a) Anchoring the mind with an object

1) External

(a) Anchoring the mind with an impure object

We perfectly assume the basic posture of the body and the gaze. As support before us, we focus our attention on a pillar, a wall, or any other form of a large size. Without being distracted by anything else, we remain evenly in this one-pointed attention. Similarly, we anchor our mind without distraction on a form of small size such as a piece of wood or a pebble placed in front of us. We may further use a butter lamp or the sky, or a white sphere of light between the eyebrows, the size of a pea, as supports of attention to anchor the mind.

(b) Anchoring the mind with a pure object

We imagine clearly before us the perfect Buddha Bhagavan. With faith and respect, we visualize the appropriate color, clothing, marks, and physical signs. Doing this with single-pointed attention, the mind is anchored.

2) Anchoring the mind internally

In the center of an eight-petalled lotus in our heart, we generate the image of a yidam of our choice, or we meditate on the lama, or we visualize a sphere of light that is their essence. Doing this the mind is anchored. In this way, we remain without distraction on the supports of attention, maintaining the position of the gaze, free of the defects of being too tense or too relaxed. Besides the awareness of a remote watch, there is nothing to do. Gentle and flexible, we rest in natural ease, without rejecting or adding anything, without hope or fear, relaxed in the relaxation.

b) Anchoring the mind without object

Either we anchor the mind first on the great emptiness of all material phenomena, external and internal, or we rest in the clear light—great emptiness after the dissolution of material phenomena into each other.

།གཏད་དམ་འབྲུང་འཛུག་གནས་གསུམ་གཅིག་རྩིས་པའི། །ཉེར་གཅིག་ལ་སོགས་གྲངས་བཟུང་མ་ཡེངས་པར། །གསལ་དངས་དར་བཙས་ཡུན་ཐུང་གྲངས་མང་འབད། །དེ་ལྟར་མན་ངག་རྣམས་ནི་སྒོམ་པའི་མཐུས། །གནས་པ་གསུམས་ལས་དང་པོ་རི་གཟར་གྱི། །ཁ་ནས་ཆུ་འབབས་དང་མཚུངས་གཉིས་པ་ནི། །ཆུ་ཀླུང་དལ་འབབས་ཐ་མ་མི་གཡོ་བ། །རྒྱ་མཚོ་ལྟ་བུ་རི་མ་གྱིས་འཆར་བར་འགྱུར། གཉིས་པ་ཟིན་པ་བརྟན་པར་བྱེད་པ་ལ། སེམས་བཅིང་བ་དང་། སེམས་གནས་པར་བྱེད་པའི་ཐབས་དགུའོ། དང་པོ་ལ། སྟེང་དུ་བཅིང་བ་དང་། འོག་ཏུ་བཅིང་བ། སྤྲོལ་མའི་རྣལ་འབྱོར་རོ། དང་པོ་ནི། །སྙིང་གར་པད་འདབ་བཞི་བའི་ལྟེ་བ་རུ། །ཐིག་ལེ་དཀར་པོ་སྲན་མ་ཙམ་ཞིག་ལ། །སེམས་འཛིན་རླུང་བཟུང་རླུང་ནི་ཕྱིར་གཏོང་མཉམ། །ཐིག་ལེ་ཚངས་བུག་ནས་སོང་ནམ་མཁའི་དབྱིངས། །གནས་པར་བསམ་ལ་ལུས་གནད་ལྟ་སྟངས་ནི། །སྙིང་དུ་གཏུན་ལ་སེམས་ནི་གཟེངས་སྟོད་ཅིང་། །རིག་པ་ཧུར་བཏོན་ཡུན་རིང་བསྒོམ་པར་བྱ། གཉིས་པ་ནི། །བཅིང་པ་བར་མ་རང་གི་སྙིང་ག་རུ། །པདྨ་ནག་པོ་འདབ་བཞི་ཁ་འོག་ཏུ། །མདོན་པར་ཕྱོགས་པའི་ལྟེ་བར་ཐིག་ལེ་ནག །སྲན་མ་ཙམ་ཞིག་བ་ཐག་བཞིན་འཕྲིལ་ནས། །གསང་བ་ནས་ཐོན་དལ་བུས་འོག་ཕྱོགས་སུ། །དཔག་ཚད་དུ་མར་ལྷུ་བའི་རྣམ་པ་ཡིས། །གནས་པར་རྩེ་གཅིག་སེམས་བཟུང་སྲིན་ཞལ་བསྡམ། །ལུས་གནད་ལྟ་སྟངས་ཐུར་དུ་དབབ་སྟེ་སྒོམ། གསུམ་པ་ནི། །གཞན་ཡང་ཚོད་དང་བསྟུན་ཏེ་སེམས་མཐོ་ན། །སྨད་དང་དེ་བཞིན་དམའ་ན་སྟོད་པ་ཡི། །དམིགས་པ་གཉིས་པོ་སྤྲོལ་མའི་རྣལ་འབྱོར་ལ། །རྟག་ཏུ་ཆུ་བོའི་རྒྱུན་བཞིན་བསྒོམ་པར་བྱ། གཉིས་པ་སེམས་གནས་པའི་ཐབས་དགུ་ནི། །འཛོག་དང་ཀུན་འཛོག་ངེས་པར་འཛོག་པ་དང་། །ཉེར་འཛོག་དུལ་བར་བྱེད་དང་ཞི་བར་བྱེད། །ཉེ་བར་ཞི་བྱེད་རྒྱུད་གཅིག་བྱེད་མཉམ་འཛོག །འདི་དག་དོན་ནི་རིམ་པ་བཞིན་དུ་བསྟན། །དམིགས་པ་གང་ལ་རྩེ་གཅིག་གཏད་དེ་འཛོག །དེ་ཉིད་ཡུན་རིང་དུ་ནི་གནས་པར་

c) Anchoring the mind with the breath

To anchor the mind with the breath, we concentrate on the vase breathing or, counting "one" for a cycle of inhaling-retaining-exhaling, we maintain our attention to a count of 21 or more cycles. With nondistraction, clarity, and stamina, we practice many short sessions.

By the power of meditating according to these instructions, the three stages of stability will gradually occur:

-the first is similar to a stream rushing down a steep mountain
-the second is similar to a quiet river
-the final stage is like a motionless ocean

2. Stabilizing the Anchored Mind

a) Fastening the mind

1) Fastening the mind above

At the center of a four-petalled lotus in our heart there is a white sphere of light the size of a pea. We fix the mind upon it, holding the breath. While we exhale, the sphere exits through the orifice of Brahma and dissolves into space. Thinking that we dwell there, we straighten the physical posture and gaze upward. As for the mind, we generate enthusiasm, and with heightened awareness, we meditate for a long duration.

2) Fastening the mind below

For the second way of fastening the mind, in the center of an upside down, black, four-petalled lotus in the heart, there is a black sphere the size of a pea. Unfolding like a spider's thread, it slowly exits the secret gate, with a sense of heaviness, going many miles down. Stabilized by this, the mind is anchored in one-pointed awareness. The buttocks need to be tightened. Meditate with a downward posture and gaze.

3) Alternating practice

In relation to the right measure, if the mind is too high, we draw it downward; if it is too low, we direct it upward. Continuously, like a flowing river, we practice the yoga of alternating these two visualizations.

b) The nine ways of stabilizing the mind

1. Settling
2. Completely settling
3. Certainly settling
4. Thoroughly settling
5. Taming
6. Pacifying
7. Thoroughly pacifying
8. Establishing one-pointedness
9. Resting evenly

ཁྲིད།[༣] །གལ་ཏེ་རྣམ་རྟོག་འཕྲོ་ན་དེ་མ་ཐག །དྲན་པས་བཟུང་སྟེ་མཉམ་པར་འཇོག[༤]པའོ། །མཉམ་པར་བཞག་པའི་སེམས་དེ་འདང་སྔར་གྱི་ནི། །གནས་པའི་སྟེང་དེར་བསྲེས་ཏེ་མཉམ་པར་འཇོག །སེམས་གནས་དེ་ཡི་ཡོན་ཏན་རྣམས་དྲན་པས། །དགའ་བ་བསྐྱེད་དེ་དེ་ཡི་ངང་དུ་གནས།[༥] །གང་ལ་འཕྲོ་བའི་རྐྱེན་དེ་དེའོ་ཞེས། །ངེས་ཤེས་དེ་ལ་ཞེན་པ་བཟློག་ཏེ[༦]གནས། །རྣམ་གཡེང་རྒྱུ་དང་ཡིད་མི་བདེ་བ་སོགས། །ངོ་བོ་ངོས་བཟུང་རང་གྲོལ་ཉིད[༧]དུ་བྱ། །དེ་ལྟར་བསྒོམས་པས་ཤུགས་ཀྱིས་དམིགས་པ་ལ། །འཇུག་ཅིང་རྩོལ་བར་མི་ལྟོས་གནས་པར[༨]ནུས། །མཐར་ནི་མཉམ་པར་བཞག་དང་མ་བཞག་པའི། །རྣམ་པར་གཡེང་བ་ཀུན་དང་བྲལ[༩]བའོ། གསུམ་པ་བརྟན་པ་ཐོགས་དབྱུང་བ་ནི། །མིག་གི་ཡུལ་དུ་སྣང་བའི་གཟུགས་རྣམས་ལ། །ཤེས་པ་གཏད་ཅིང་དེ་བཞིན་སྒྲ་སོགས་ལའང་། །རིམ་གྱིས་དམིགས་རྟེན་བྱས་ནས་རྩེ་གཅིག་བཞག །དེ་ཡང་རྣམ་པར་རྟོག་པ་གང་སྐྱེས་ཀྱང་། །སྐྱོན་དུ་མི་བལྟ་དེ་ཐོག་ཅོན་གྱིས་བཞག །སྒྲིམས་ལྷོད་གཉིས་སྤེལ་ཁྱད་པར་གེགས་སེལ་དང་། །ཐོགས་འདོན་མཆོག་གསུམ་བླ་མར་གསོལ་འདེབས་དང་། །མོས་གུས་སྒོ་ནས་ཐུགས་ཡིད་གཅིག་ཏུ་བསྲེས། གཉིས་པ་ལྷག་མཐོང་ལ། གནས་ལུགས་སེམས་ཀྱི་ངོ་བོ་ལ་བལྟ་བ་དང་། གཞི་རྩ་གཅོད་པ། རིག་སྟོང་དུ་གཏན་ལ་ཕབ་ནས་ངོ་སྤྲོད་པའོ། དང་པོ་ནི། །གནས་ལུགས་སེམས་ཀྱི་ངོ་བོར་བལྟ་བའི་ཚུལ། །རང་བབས་མ་བཅོས་ལྷོད་ཀྱི་གློད་ནས་འཇོག །ངོ་བོ་ཁ་དོག་གཟུགས་དབྱིབས་སོགས་ཇི་ལྟར། །གཞིག་ཅིང་དཔྱོད་ལ་ཡང་ནས་ཡང་དུ་ལྟོས། །གནས་པ་དེ་ཡི་ངོ་བོ་ཇི་ལྟར་ན། །གསལ་ཞིང་ཧྲིག་གེ་བ་ལ་རྗེན་ནེར་དགོས། །གལ་ཏེ་གནས་པ་བཙལ་བས་མ་རྙེད་ན། །འཕྲོ་རུ་བཅུག་ལ་ཇི་ལྟར་འཕྲོ་ཞིང་དཔྱོད། གཉིས་པ་ནི། །དེ་ནས་གཞི་རྩ་གཅོད་པའི་ཚུལ་བསྟན་པར། །བཙལ་ཚེ་མ་རྙེད་པ་ན་འཚོལ་མཁན་དང་། །སེམས་དེའི་བྱུང་གནས་འགྲོ་གསུམ་སོགས་ཇི་ལྟར། །ལེགས་པར་བརྟག་ནས་ཡང་ཡང་བཙལ་བར་བྱ།

These skillful means are explained as follows:
1. Settling: placing one pointed attention on any object
2. Completely settling: keeping the previous stability for a long duration
3. Certainly settling: if thoughts occur, they are identified immediately by awareness, then resting evenly.
4. Thoroughly settling: in addition to having previously settled the stabilized mind, clarifying it, and then resting evenly.
5. Taming: remembering perfectly the qualities of the stabilized mind, generating joy, and remaining in this state.
6. Pacifying: identifying the cause of any production [of thought], whatever it is by "Here it is!" Being certain to have discovered it, turning away from the attraction.
7. Thoroughly pacifying: identifying the causes of distraction and the essence of unhappy states, and so on; they are spontaneously liberated; remaining stable.
8. Establishing one-pointedness: having the ability to remain stable while contemplating the object by the power of a familiarization disregarding effort.
9. Resting evenly: finally, staying free of all distractions whether resting evenly or not [in meditation].

3. Enhancing the Stability

We direct the awareness to forms which appear as visual objects, then sounds, and so on, using them successively as supports of awareness. We settle our mind on them with one-pointedness. In the same way, whatever thoughts arise, we do not look at them as defects, but instantly, we settle our mind on them. To remove tension and sloth, and most particularly, to dispel obstacles and enhance the practice, the best way is to pray to the lama, and through devotion, blend our mind and the lamas's mind into one.

II. Superior Vision [Lhakthong]

1. Observing the Mode of Being, the Essence of the Mind

The way to observe the essential nature of the mind is to leave the mind in natural ease, in nondoing, relaxed in relaxation. We look again and again, examining and analyzing it. What is its essence, color, shape, form, size, and so on? If we ask what this essence of the stable mind is, it must be clarity, presence, and bareness. When we look for stability and do not find it, then, we should let the production (of thoughts) arise and examine it.

།གཞན་ཡང་ཡིད་ལ་བྱེད་པ་བཅུ་གཅིག་སྟེ། །ཡོངས་སུ་ཚོལ་རབ་བྱེད་པ་དང་སོ་སོར་བརྟག
།ཞིབ་མོར་དཔྱོད་པ་ཞི་གནས་ལྷག་མཐོང་དང་། །ཟུང་འབྲེལ་གསལ་བ་མི་རྟོག་བདུད་རྩི་སྒོམ
དང་། །རྒྱུན་མི་ཆད་པ་ཡེངས་པ་མེད་རབ་བྱེད། །འདི་རྣམས་དོན་ནི་རིམ་པ་བཞིན་བསྟན་ཏེ།
།སེམས་ནི་ཡོད་མེད་ངོ་བོ་ཇི་ལྟར་ཞེས། སེམས་ཀྱི་རྒྱུད་ལ་བྲེང་ཆགས་སུ་ནི་བཙལ། །ཁྱད
པར་ཁ་དོག་དང་ནི་དབྱིབས་ལ་སོགས། །བྱུང་གནས་འགྲོ་གསུམ་གཞི་རྟེན་རྩད་གཅོད་དོ།
།ཚོལ་པོ་ཚོལ་མཁན་མཐར་ནི་ཐུག་པར་བཙལ། །བཙལ་བས་རང་སེམས་རང་བཞིན་མེད
རྟོགས་སུ་པས། །ཆོས་ཀུན་གནས་ལུགས་ཀྱང་ནི་གཏན་ཕེབ་ཕྱིར། །ཟབ་མོའི་དོན་ལ་སེམས་ནི་ཉི
བརྟུ་གནས། །གནས་པ་དེ་ཉིད་ངོ་བོ་སྤྱི་མ་ལྟར། །བཙལ་བས་རང་ངོ་ཡོངས་སུ་རྟོགས་སུ་པའོ།
།དེ་དག་ཐ་དད་མ་ཡིན་དབྱེར་མི་ཕྱེད། །གལ་ཏེ་བྱིང་ཞིང་རྨུགས་པར་གྱུར་པ་ན། །རྒོད་རྒྱུ
ཡིད་ལ་བྱ་ཞིང་སེམས་གཟེངས་སུ་བསྟོད། །འཕྲོ་རྒོད་གྱུར་ན་ཞི་བའི་ཐབས་ལ་འབད། །བྱིང་རྒོད
བྲལ་བར་གྱུར་པའི་གནས་སྐབས་སུ། །ཚུལ་བརྟག་དཔྱད་པའི་ངོ་བོར་གནས་པར་བྱ། །དེ་ལྟའི
རྣལ་འབྱོར་ནམ་ཡང་མི་འབྲལ་བྱ། །དེ་ལ་སེམས་ནི་ཉི་བར་བསྒྲིམས་བྱས་ནས། །རྣམ་པར
གཡེང་བས་གླགས་མི་རྙེད་པར་བྱ། །དེ་ལྟར་ཡིད་བྱེད་བཅུ་གཅིག་སྒོ་ནས་ཀྱང་། །གཞི་རྩ
གཅད་པའི་ཚུལ་ལ་ཡང་ཡང་འབད། གསུམ་པ་ནི། །རིག་སྟོང་གཏན་ལ་ཕབ་ནས་ངོ་སྤྲོད་ཚུལ།
།ཐོག་མར་སེམས་ནི་རང་ལུགས་གློད་ལ་ཞོག །གློད་པའི་སེམས་ཀྱི་ངོ་བོར་ཇེན་ནེར་ལྟོས།
།མ་ཡེངས་ཙམ་གྱི་དྲན་པ་རྒྱུན་ཆགས་བསྟེན། །རྣམ་རྟོག་གང་ཤར་ཆེད་དུ་སྤང་བླང་དང་།
།བཅས་བཅོས་གང་ཡང་མི་བྱེད་ཐ་མལ་གྱི། །ཤེས་པ་སྐད་ཅིག་ངོས་བཟུང་དང་བྲལ་བའི།
།གསལ་སྟོང་ལྷང་ངེ་བ་ལ་ཧྲིག་གེར་ཞོག ཡང་ངོ་སྤྲོད་གདབ་ཚུལ་ལ། འགྱུ་ཐོག་ནས་ངོ་སྤྲོད་པ་དང་། སྣང
ཐོག་ནས་ངོ་སྤྲོད་པ་གཉིས་ལས། དང་པོ་ནི། །གཞན་ཡང་འགྱུ་ཐོག་ནས་ནི་ངོ་སྤྲོད་ཚུལ། །ཐོག་མར

2. Cutting Uncertainty

Here is how to cut uncertainty. When we search, if we do not find anything, who is the one searching? How does the mind arise, dwell, and disappear? Perfectly examining, we must continuously search.

There are the 11 recollections.

1. thorough search and analysis
2. separate analysis
3. detailed analysis
4. mental calming [shinay]
5. superior vision [lhakthong]
6. combining both
7. clarity
8. nonthought
9. equanimity
10. noninterruption
11. nondistraction

The explanation of each of these points is as follows.

1. Does the mind exist or not? What is its essence? We search in the stream of mind, which is continuity.
2. In particular, we eliminate doubts about its color, shape, and so on, its origin, location, and disappearance.
3. The searcher searches, up to the end, the one who searches.
4. Realizing through searching that the mind lacks an inherent nature, the mind remains perfectly stable in the profound meaning in order to also arrive at a conclusion about the essential nature of all phenomena.
5. Searching as before for the essence of that which remains stable, we realize its own face completely.
6. The two preceding [points] are neither different nor dissociated.
7. If through torpor, obscuration occurs, we revitalize the mind by producing causes of agitation.
8. If production [of thoughts] and agitation occur, we apply the methods for calming.
9. When we are free from torpor and agitation, we remain in the essence of the one who is searching, examining, and analyzing.
10. Never be separated from this yoga.
11. Perfectly maintained in this yoga, the mind has no occasion to be distracted.

Through these 11 recollections, we continuously apply the methods that cut away uncertainty.

ཤེས་པ་རང་ལུགས་གློད་ནས་བཞག ། དེ་ཡི་ངང་ནས་རང་གི་ངོ་བོ་བལྟ། ། དེ་ནས་འགྱུར་བཅུག་སླར་ཡང་འགྱུ་མཁན་སེམས། དེ་དང་གནས་པའི་སེམས་ལ་ཁྱད་པར་ཅི། །འགྱུ་སེམས་དེ་དང་དེ་ལ་བལྟ་བའི་སེམས། །ཁྱད་པར་བལྟས་པས་འགྱུ་བ་རང་གྲོལ་འགྲོ། །དེ་ཡི་ངང་དུ་མ་ཡེངས་རྩེ་གཅིག་ཞོག གཉིས་པ་སྣང་ཐོག་ནས་ངོ་སྤྲོད་པ་ལ། སྣང་བ་སེམས། སེམས་སྟོང་པ། སྟོང་པ་ལྷུན་གྲུབ། ལྷུན་གྲུབ་རང་གྲོལ་དུ་ངོ་སྤྲོད་པ་རྣམས་ལས། དང་པོ་ནི། །གཟུགས་སོགས་དམིགས་པའི་རྟེན་བྱས་དེ་དང་སེམས། །གཅིག་གམ་ཐ་དད་བརྟག་པས་ཕྱི་རོལ་གྱི། །སྣང་བའི་ཡུལ་ཀུན་སེམས་ཀྱི་རང་མདངས་ལས། །གཞན་དུ་གྲུབ་པ་མེད་པར་རྟོགས་གྱུར་ན། །དེ་ཡི་ངང་དུ་འཛིན་མེད་ཕྱད་དེ་ཞོག གཉིས་པ་སེམས་སྟོང་པར་ངོ་སྤྲོད་པ་ནི། སེམས་ཉིད་ཅིར་ཡང་མ་གྲུབ་སྟོང་པ་ཉིད། །དེ་ནི་གང་གིས་ཀྱང་ནི་མཚོན་དུ་མེད། །སྨྲ་བསམ་བརྗོད་བྲལ་ནམ་མཁའ་ལྟ་བུ་སྟེ། །དེ་ཡི་ངང་དུ་མ་བཅོས་ལྷུག་པར་ཞོག གསུམ་པ་སྟོང་པ་ལྷུན་གྲུབ་ཏུ་ངོ་སྤྲོད་པ་ནི། །སྟོང་པའི་ཆོས་ལས་གཡོ་བ་མེད་བཞིན་དུ། །རྩལ་མདངས་མ་འགགས་སྣ་ཚོགས་འཆར་བ་ཉིད། །སྟོང་ལས་གཞན་མེད་སྣང་སྲིད་འཁོར་འདས་ཆོས། །ལྷུན་གྲུབ་སྣང་སྟོང་དབྱེར་མེད་ཉིད་རིག་བྱ། བཞི་པ་ལྷུན་གྲུབ་རང་གྲོལ་དུ་ངོ་སྤྲོད་པ་ནི། དེ་བཞིན་སྣང་རིག་སྟོང་གསུམ་གདོད་མ་ནས། །གསལ་སྟོང་ཟུང་འཇུག་ལྷུན་གྱིས་གྲུབ་པ་ལ། །སྤང་བླང་བསལ་བཞག་གཉེན་པོར་མ་ལྟོས་པར། །དོན་གྱི་རང་གྲོལ་ཕྱག་རྒྱ་ཆེན་པོའོ། གསུམ་པ་རྗེས་ཀྱི་དོན་ལ། རང་གི་ངོ་བོ་བླ་མས་ངོ་སྤྲད་པ། དེ་ཉམས་སུ་མྱོང་ནས་རྩལ་སྦྱངས་ཤིང་བོགས་འདོན་པའི་ཚུལ་དང་། གེགས་བསལ་བ། ལམ་བགྲོད་ཚུལ། འབྲས་བུ་མངོན་དུ་བྱེད་ཚུལ་དང་བཞི་ལས། དང་པོ་ལོག་རྟོག་ལྟ་བསལ་ཏེ་བོགས་འདོན་པ་ལས། དང་པོ་ཡུལ་ལ་ལོག་རྟོག་བསལ་ཚུལ་ནི། །འཁོར་བ་སྤང་བྱ་མྱ་ངན་འདས་བསྒྲུབ་བྱར། །ཨ་འཐས་ཞེན་འཛིན་མེད་པར་དགེ་སྡིག་སོགས། །གཉིས་བསྡུས་ཆོས་ཀུན་གཉིས་མེད་ཡེ་ཤེས་དབྱིངས། །རོ་མཉམ་བྱས་པས་ཡུལ་ལ་ལོག་རྟོག་སེལ། གཉིས་པ་དུས་ལ

3. Pointing Out Instructions to Conclude That Awareness Is Emptiness

The instructions to conclude that awareness is empty are like this. First, we place the relaxed mind in its own nature. We look at the essence of this relaxed mind in its bareness. We maintain one pointed awareness that is simply nondistracted. Whatever thoughts arise, we do not reject them or intentionally accept them. We do not mentally create anything but rest vividly and openly in ordinary mind, in the instant, and in a clarity without identification.

Additional ways of pointing out.

a) Pointing out through movement

The way of pointing out through movement is first to let the mind settle in its own nature in a relaxed way. In this state, we look at its own essence. Then, we induce a movement. What is then the difference between the moving mind and the stable mind? What is the difference between the moving mind and the mind that observes it? Observing like this, the movement is spontaneously liberated. We dwell without distraction and with one pointed attention in this state.

b) Pointing out through appearances

1) Pointing out appearances as mind

We examine whether the forms and other supports of objective perception are one with the mind or are different. When we realize that all objects which externally appear have no existence except as reflections of the mind, we continually rest in this state without fixation.

2) Pointing out mind as emptiness

The mind in itself is nothing existing but emptiness. It can be illustrated by nothing. Beyond word, thought, description, it is like space. We dwell relaxed in this state, without fabrication.

3) Pointing out emptiness as spontaneous presence

Manifestation, radiance, and unimpededness arise in diversity, unmoving from the domain of emptiness. We must understand that there is nothing but emptiness; all appearances, all phenomena of samsara and nirvana are the spontaneous presence of inseparable appearance and emptiness.

4) Pointing out self-liberation as spontaneous presence

Likewise, appearances, awareness, and emptiness are primordially the spontaneous presence of the union of clarity and emptiness. With no need for antidotes that reject, take, disregard, or establish, this is the self-liberation of reality, the Mahamudra.

ལོག་རྟོག་བསལ་ཚུལ་ནི། །དུས་གསུམ་བདེན་དངོས་གྲུབ་པ་མེད་བཞིན་དུ། །དུས་གསུམ་དབྱེ་བ
རྨོངས་པས་བཏགས་པ་སྟེ། །དེ་ཕྱིར་དུས་གསུམ་ཐ་དད་མ་གྲུབ་པར། །མཉམ་ཉིད་རྟོགས་པ
དུས་ལ་ལོག་རྟོག་སེལ། གསུམ་པ་ངོ་བོ་ལ་ལོག་རྟོག་བསལ་ཚུལ་ནི། །ད་ལྟའི་སེམས་འདི་སྣང་ནས་ཕྱིས
ཡེ་ཤེས། །ཐོབ་པར་འདོད་པ་ཕྱིན་ཅི་ལོག་པ་སྟེ། །རང་སེམས་གདོད་ནས་ཡེ་ཤེས་ལྷའི་རང་
བཞིན། །ཡིན་པར་ཤེས་པ་ངོ་བོར་ལོག་རྟོག་སེལ། བཞི་པ་རང་བཞིན་ལ་ལོག་རྟོག་བསལ་ཚུལ་ནི།
།སེམས་ཅན་རྣམས་ཀྱི་ཕུང་ཁམས་སྐྱེ་མཆེད་ཀུན། །གདོད་ནས་དེ་བཞིན་གཤེགས་པ
གཤེགས་མ་དང་། །ལྷ་དང་ལྷ་མོའི་རང་བཞིན་ཉིད་གནས་པ། །དེ་ལྟར་ཤེས་པ་རང་བཞིན
ལོག་རྟོག་སེལ། ལྔ་པ་ཤེས་རབ་ལ་ལོག་རྟོག་བསལ་ཚུལ་ནི། །དམ་པའི་དོན་ནི་ཤེས་རབ་ཆེ་བ་དང་།
རྟོག་གེའི་ཡུལ་མིན་བླ་མའི་བྱིན་རླབས་དང་། །སྐལ་ལྡན་ལས་འཕྲོ་ཅན་གྱིས་རྟོགས་པ་སྟེ།
།དེ་ནི་ཤེས་རབ་ལ་ནི་ལོག་རྟོག་སེལ། གཉིས་པ་མཁས་པ་གསུམ་ལ་སློབ་པ་སྟེ། དང་པོ་སྒོམ་གྱི་མགོ་རྩོམ་པ་ལ
མཁས་པ། བར་དུ་སྒོམ་གྱི་འཕྲོ་བཅོད་པ་ལ་མཁས་པ། མཐར་ཉམས་བསྐྱང་བ་ལ་མཁས་པ་དང་བཅས་སོ། དང་པོ་ནི།
།ལུས་གནད་ལེགས་བཅས་འཕྲོ་ན་འཕྲོ་ཐོག་དང་། །གནས་ན་གནས་ཐོག་ངོ་བོ་ལ་བལྟས་ཏེ།
།མ་བཅོས་སོ་མ་ལྷུག་པ་རང་བབས་དང་། །མ་ཡེངས་རང་ངོ་ཤེས་ཙམ་ཐོག་ཏུ་ཞོག གཉིས་པ་ནི།
།གང་ལ་མཉམ་བཞག་རྒྱུན་རིང་གཙོར་མི་འདོན། །ཏིང་ངེ་འཛིན་དང་ལུས་གནད་རྣམས
བསྲུར་ཞིང་། །ཡུན་ཐུང་གྲངས་མང་གསལ་དངས་ངར་བཅས་ཏེ། །སྒོམ་དང་འཕོན་གྱིས་མ
སོང་བྲིད་པ་བསྐྱེད། གསུམ་པ་ནི། །བདེ་གསལ་མི་རྟོག་ཉམས་གསུམ་གང་ཤར་ཡང་། །ཆགས
ཞེན་ང་རྒྱལ་སྐྱེས་ན་ཉམས་ཀྱི་ཕྱིར། །རྟོགས་པ་ཤོར་བ་ཞེས་བྱ་དེ་བས་ནི། །ཉམས་ལ་ཞེན་པ
བྲལ་བའི་ངང་ནས་སྐྱོངས། གསུམ་པ་ཤོར་ས་དང་གོལ་ས་བཅད་དེ་བོགས་འདོན་པ་ནི། །དང་པོ་ཤོར་ས་ལ། སྟོང་
ཉིད་ཤེས་བྱའི་གཤིས་ལ་ཤོར་བ་དང་། རྒྱས་འདེབས་སུ་ཤོར་བ། གཉེན་པོར་ཤོར་བ། ལམ་དུ་ཤོར་བ་དང་བཞི་ལས། དང་

Post-Practice

After we have experienced our own essence as pointed out by the lama, we enhance and refine this experience, dispel hindrances, tread the path, and actualize the result.

I. ENHANCEMENT

1. Enhancement through Eliminating Five False Ideas

a) How to eliminate false ideas about objects

Without grasping something real in the notion of samsara that must be abandoned and nirvana that must be actualized, but placing ourselves in the infinite one-taste of primordial awareness [of knowing] the nonduality of all phenomena gathered by pairs such as virtue and nonvirtue, we eliminate false ideas about objects.

b) How to eliminate false ideas about time

Although there is no fundamental truth about the reality of the three times, we think within a mode obscured by the division into three times. Consequently, realizing equanimity which does not establish a distinction of the three times, we eliminate the false ideas about time.

c) How to eliminate false ideas about essence

We have a mistaken desire to abandon this present mind to obtain an external primordial awareness. Recognizing that our mind is originally of the nature of the five wisdoms, we eliminate the false ideas about essence.

d) How to eliminate false ideas about nature

All aggregates, elements, and systems of perception of beings are primordially of the nature of the masculine and feminine tathagatas and deities. Recognizing this, we eliminate false ideas about nature.

e) How to eliminate false ideas about knowledge

Absolute truth is no object of great intelligence or analytical discourse. It is realized through the grace of the lama and with favorable karmic potential. In this way, the false ideas about knowledge are eliminated.

2. Training in the Three Skills

a) Skillfulness in beginning meditation

We place our body in the basic posture. If [thoughts] arise, we look at the essence of the production [of thoughts]; if the mind is stable, we look at the essence of the stability. We remain in a state of natural ease, nonfabrication, freshness, relaxation, in the simple recognition of our own essence, without distraction.

པོ་ནི། །ལུང་རིགས་ཐོས་བསམ་ཐ་སྙད་ཀྱི་སྒོ་ནས། །དངོས་པོའི་གནས་ལུགས་སྟོང་པར་གཏན་
ཕབ་ཅིང་། །ཐམས་ཅད་སྟོང་པས་སྒོམ་རྒྱུ་ཅི་ཡོད་ཅེས། །བློས་བྱས་སྒོ་ནས་འཛོག་ཕྱིར་ཡང་
དག་མིན། གཉིས་པ་ནི། །སྟོང་ཉིད་རྒྱུས་འདེབས་ཤོར་ཞེས་དངོས་པོ་ཀུན། །སྟོང་ཉིད་མ་ཡིན་
པར་བཟུང་ཤཱུ་ནྱ་ཏའི། །སྔགས་སོགས་བརྗོད་པས་སྟོང་པར་སོང་སྙམ་ཏེ། །སྒོམ་པར་བྱེད་པའང་
ཡང་དག་མ་ཡིན་ནོ། གསུམ་པ་ནི། །སྟོང་ཉིད་གཉེན་པོར་ཤོར་ཞེས་དུག་གསུམ་སོགས། །རྣམ་
རྟོག་སྐྱེས་ཚེ་འདི་རྣམས་སྟོང་ཉིད་ཀྱིས། །གཞོམ་པར་བྱའོ་སྙམ་སྟེ་སྟོང་ཉིད་དུ། །མཉམ་པར་
འཛོག་པ་དེ་ནི་དྲི་མ་ཅན། བཞི་པ་ནི། །སྟོང་ཉིད་ལམ་དུ་ཤོར་ཞེས་སྟོང་ཉིད་ལ། །ལམ་དང་
འབྲས་བུ་གཉིས་སུ་མེད་བཞིན་དུ། ད་ལྟ་སྟོང་ཉིད་སྒོམ་པ་དེས་ལམ་བྱས། །ཕྱི་ནས་འབྲས་བུ་
ཐོབ་སྙམ་ཡང་དག་མིན། གཉིས་པ་སྒོམ་པའི་གོལ་ས་བཅད་དེ་བོགས་འདོན་པ་ནི། །དེ་བཞིན་གོལ་ས་བཅད་
དེ་བོགས་འདོན་ཚུལ། །རྣམ་གྲངས་བཅུ་བདུན་རིམ་བཞིན་བསྟན་པར་བྱ། །བདེ་གསལ་མི་
རྟོག་གསུམ་ལས་བདེ་ཉམས་ལ། །ཟག་བཅས་ཟག་མེད་སོ་སོར་མ་ཕྱེ་བར། །སྲིད་ཀྱི་བདེ་ལ་
ཤེས་རབ་ཀྱིས་བརྟགས་པ། །དེ་ཉིད་བསྒོམས་ནས་ཡང་དག་ཞེན་གྱུར་ན། །འདོད་པའི་ཁམས་
སུ་གོལ་ཞིང་དེ་བཞིན་དུ། །གསལ་བའི་ཉམས་ལ་ཞེན་ན་གཟུགས་ཁམས་གོལ། །མི་རྟོག་པ་
ལ་ཞེན་ན་གཟུགས་མེད་སྐྱེ། །དེ་ལའང་ཆོས་ཀུན་ནམ་མཁའ་དང་འདྲ་ཞེས། །ཤེས་རབ་ཀྱིས་
དཔྱད་ཡང་དག་ཞེན་གྱུར་ན། །ནམ་མཁའ་མཐའ་ཡས་སྐྱེ་མཆེད་ཉིད་དུ་སྐྱེ། །ཆོས་རྣམས་
སེམས་ཡིན་སྙམ་དུ་བཟུང་བ་ལས། །རྣམ་ཤེས་མཐའ་ཡས་སྐྱེ་མཆེད་ལ་ནི་གོལ། །ཅི་ཡང་མ་
གྲུབ་སྙམ་དུ་ཞེན་པས་ན། །ཅི་ཡང་མེད་པའི་སྐྱེ་མཆེད་ཉིད་དུ་གོལ། །ཡོད་མིན་མེད་མིན་སྙམ་
དུ་ཞེན་གྱུར་ན། །འདུ་ཤེས་མེད་མིན་སྐྱེ་མཆེད་ལ་ནི་སྐྱེ། །དེས་ན་བདེ་གསལ་མི་རྟོག་ཉམས་
རྣམས་ལ། །ཆགས་ཞེན་དང་བྲལ་རང་ཞལ་མཐོང་བས་སེལ། །ཐབས་དང་བྲལ་ཞིང་སྟོང་པར་

b) Skillfulness in ending meditation

Not considering it essential to meditate for long periods of time, but modifying the methods of meditation and physical posture, we do many short sessions keeping the mind clear, radiant, and vivid. Not ending the meditation in resentment, we generate enthusiasm.

c) Skillfulness in maintaining meditation

Whenever experiences of joy, clarity, and nonthought occur, if we conceive attachment or pride, it is called losing realization to the experience. It is therefore necessary to maintain [the meditation] in a state without attachment to the experience.

3. ENHANCEMENT THROUGH ELIMINATING MISTAKES AND WANDERINGS

a) Mistakes

1) Mistaking emptiness, the nature of objects of knowledge

Studying scriptures and sciences, we conclude through reasoning that the essential nature of matter is empty. We think, "Since everything is empty, on what are we to meditate?" If emptiness is established only intellectually, it is not authentic emptiness.

2) Mistaking the seal

What is called mistaking the seal of emptiness is when we think that all material phenomena that we do not perceive as empty are made empty by reciting mantras such as the mantra called sunyata. This is only a meditation; it is not authentic emptiness.

3) Mistaking the antidote

What is called mistaking emptiness as the antidote is when thoughts occur and we think, "I will conquer them by emptiness." This way of being placed in emptiness is stained.

4) Mistaking the path

What is called mistaking emptiness as the path is thinking that treading the path with meditation on emptiness now—although path and result are not separated—we will obtain the result later. This is not authentic.

b) Enhancement through eliminating wandering while meditating

The way of enhancement through eliminating wandering will be shown in 17 successive points.

1. Among the three types of experiences—joy, clarity, and nonthought—let us take the example of joy. While not distinguishing between conditioned and nonconditioned joy, we generally examine this joy through knowledge. If, meditating on this joy, a true attachment occurs, it is wandering in the desire realm.

ཞེན་གྱུར་ན། །དམན་པར་གོལ་བས་དེ་ཉིད་སྤྱོད་པའི་ཚུལ། །བརྩེ་བ་སྙིང་རྗེ་བྱང་ཆུབ་སེམས་
བསྒོམ་བྱ། །ཐབས་ཀྱིས་ཤེས་རབ་བོགས་འདོན་ཤེས་རབ་ཀྱིས། །ཐབས་ཀྱི་བོགས་འདོན་དེ་
གཉིས་ཟུང་འཇུག་གིས། །གཅིག་གི་བོགས་འདོན་གཅིག་ཤོས་འདོན་པར་བྱ། །ཞི་གནས་
བོགས་ནི་ལྷག་མཐོང་གིས་འདོན་ཞིང་། །ལྷག་མཐོང་བོགས་ཀྱང་ཞི་གནས་ཀྱིས་འདོན་བྱ།
།ཞི་གནས་ལྷག་མཐོང་གཉིས་པོ་རྩེ་གཅིག་ལ། །ཉམས་ཀྱི་བོགས་ནི་ཉམས་ཀྱིས་འདོན་པར་
བྱ། །དེ་བཞིན་སྤྲོས་བྲལ་ལ་ནི་རྟོགས་པའི་བོགས། །ཉམས་ཀྱིས་འདོན་པར་བྱ་ཞིང་རོ་གཅིག་
ལ། །རྟོགས་པའི་བོགས་ནི་རྟོགས་པས་འདོན་པར་བྱ། །སྒོ་གསུམ་ཐ་མལ་དུ་ནི་མ་ལུས་པར།
།ཅི་བྱེད་དགེ་བའི་ཡོ་ལང་ཉིད་བསྒྱུར་ནས། །ཐ་མལ་ཡོན་ཏན་དུ་ནི་བོགས་འདོན་བྱ། །ཉོན་
མོངས་སྡུག་བསྔལ་བར་ཆད་ལ་སོགས་སྐྱོན། །སྤང་བླང་མེད་པར་རང་ཞལ་ལ་བལྟས་ནས།
།ལྟས་ངན་གཡང་དུ་ལེན་ནས་བོགས་འདོན་ནོ། བཞི་པ་འཕྲང་གསུམ་བསྒྲལ་ཏེ་བོགས་འདོན་པ་ལ། སྟོང་པ་
དགྲར་ལངས་དང་། སྙིང་རྗེ་དགྲར་ལངས་དང་། རྒྱུ་འབྲས་དགྲར་ལངས་དང་གསུམ་ལས། དང་པོ་ནི། །སེམས་ཀྱི་ངོ་
བོར་དཔྱད་ཅིང་བལྟས་པའི་ཚེ། །ཅི་ཡང་མ་གྲུབ་མཐོང་བས་ཆོས་ཐམས་ཅད། །སྟོང་ཉིད་ཁོ་ན
ཡིན་ཕྱིར་དགེ་སྡིག་དང་། །རྒྱུ་འབྲས་སོགས་ཀྱང་གྲུབ་པ་མེད་སྙམ་སྟེ། །སྤང་གཉེན་མི་བཟུང་
ནག་པོ་ཁ་འབྱམས་ཞེས། །སྟོང་པ་དགྲར་ལངས་ཡིན་ཏེ་དུག་ལྟར་སྤོངས། གཉིས་པ་ནི། །བདག
ཉིད་ཏིང་འཛིན་བདེ་བ་ཙུང་ཟད་ཙམ། །ཐོབ་པས་དེ་དང་མི་ལྡན་སེམས་ཅན་རྣམས། །གྲོལ་བར་
བྱ་སྙམ་རང་གི་ཏིང་དེ་འཛིན། །ངོར་ནས་རྩོལ་བ་དང་བཅས་འདུས་བྱས་ཀྱི། །དགེ་ལ་འཇུག
ཅིང་བདེན་པར་ཞེན་པ་ནི། །སྙིང་རྗེ་དགྲར་ལངས་ཞེས་བྱ་དེ་སྤང་སྟེ། །སྙིང་རྗེ་སྐྱེས་པ་དེ་དང་
འབྲལ་མེད་དང་། །རང་གི་རྟོགས་པ་དབྱེ་མེད་སྐྱོང་ལ་འབད། གསུམ་པ་ནི། །གནས་ལུགས་ཟབ་
མོ་མཐོང་བར་བྱེད་པ་ལ། །ཤེས་བྱ་ཀུན་ལ་མཁས་པར་དགོས་སྙམ་སྟེ། །སྒྲ་ཚད་སོགས་ལ་

2. In the same way, if attachment to the experience of clarity occurs, it is wandering in the form realm.
3. If attachment to nonthought occurs, we will take rebirth in the formless realm. It is said that there all phenomena are similar to space. If, analyzing this through knowledge, a thorough attachment occurs, we will take rebirth in the system of perception of limitless space.
4. From clinging to the idea that all phenomena are mind, we wander in the system of perception of limitless individual consciousness.
5. If attached to the idea that nothing exists, we wander in the system of perception of nothing whatsoever.
6. If attachment to the idea that neither existence nor nonexistence occurs, we will take rebirth in the system of perception of neither discrimination nor nondiscrimination.
Consequently, let us eliminate these wanderings by being free of attachment to the experiences of joy, clarity, and nonthought, but by seeing our own face.
7. If there is attachment to emptiness separated from skillful means, we then wander in inferior states. The way to reject this is to develop love, compassion, and the mind of Awakening.
8. Through skillful means, we enhance wisdom.
9. Through wisdom, we enhance skillful means.
10. By integrating both, enhancing one we will enhance the other.
11. Enhancing mental calming is done by superior vision.
12. Enhancing superior vision is done by mental calming.
13. At the level of one-pointedness, for both mental calming and superior vision, enhancement of the experience is done by experience.
14. At the level of nonfabrication, enhancement of the realization is done by experience.
15. At the level of one taste, enhancement of the realization is done by realization.
16. Without rejecting the three gates as being ordinary, anything we do is transformed into virtue; ordinary qualities are enhanced.
17. Without rejecting or accepting defects such as conflicting emotions, suffering, and obstacles, we look at our own face. Enhancement is done by taking bad omens as blessings.

4. Enhancement Through Liberation from the Three Perilous Paths

a) Emptiness arising as an enemy

When we analyze and examine the essence of the mind, we see nothing existing. Since all phenomena are empty, we think that positive and negative acts, as well as the law of karma, do not exist. Considering that there is nothing to reject and no antidote to apply is called nihilism. As emptiness arises as an enemy, we reject this thought like poison.

འཇུག་ཅིང་ཞི་ལྷག་གི། །རྣལ་འབྱོར་དོར་བར་བྱེད་ན་རྒྱུ་འབྲས་ཀྱི། །རྟོག་པ་དགྲར་ལངས་ཞེས་བྱ་ཡང་དག་མིན། །དེ་ཕྱིར་ཟབ་མོའི་དོན་ལ་རྩེ་གཅིག་ཏུ། །བསྒོམས་པས་སྣང་སྲིད་འཁོར་འདས་ཆོས་ཀུན་ལ། །རྨོངས་པ་མེད་པའི་དྲི་མེད་ཤེས་རབ་ཐོབ། གཉིས་པ་གེགས་སེལ་ལ། ནད་དང་གདོན་དང་། ཏིང་ངེ་འཛིན་གྱི་གེགས་སེལ་གསུམ་ལས། དང་པོ་ནི། །ཞི་གནས་གཙོ་བོར་བསྒོམས་པས་རླུང་ནད་སེལ། །ལྷག་མཐོང་བསྒོམས་པས་བད་འཁྲིས་ནད་དག་སེལ། །ཡང་ན་ཚ་གྲང་ནད་གཉིས་ཞི་ལྷག་གིས། །རིམ་གྱིས་སེལ་ཞིང་དེ་བཞིན་ནད་གང་གི །ངོ་བོ་དབྱིབས་དང་བྱུང་གནས་འགྲོ་གསུམ་བརྟགས། །ཁྱད་པར་གཏོང་ལེན་དམིགས་པར་ནན་ཏན་བྱ། །ཡང་ན་ནད་ནི་སྐྱེ་མེད་ཆོས་ཀྱི་སྐུ། །གནས་མེད་ལོངས་སྐུ་འགག་པ་མེད་སྤྲུལ་སྐུ། །རང་བཞིན་སྟོང་པ་ངོ་བོ་ཉིད་སྐུ་སྟེ། །སྐུ་བཞིའི་རོལ་པར་ཁྱེར་ཏེ་རང་ཞལ་ལྟོས། གཉིས་པ་ནི། །དེ་བཞིན་གདོན་གྱི་གེགས་སེལ་ཚུལ་ལ་ཡང་། །གདོན་དུ་སྣང་བ་སེམས་ཀྱི་ཆོ་འཕྲུལ་ཏེ། །སེམས་ཉིད་སྐུ་བཞིར་ཁྱེར་ལ་གདོན་དེ་ཡང་། །སྐུ་བཞིའི་ལམ་དུ་ཁྱེར་བའི་སྒོ་ནས་སེལ། གསུམ་པ་ནི། །སྤྱིར་ན་བྱིང་རྒོད་སྒྲོན་སེལ་སྔར་བསྟན་བཞིན། །འདི་ན་བླ་མའི་རྣལ་འབྱོར་གྱིས་སེལ་ན། །བྱིང་ཚེ་སྤྱི་བོར་བླ་མ་འོད་དཔག་མེད། །དེ་ལ་བརྒྱུད་པའི་བླ་མ་སོགས་བསྡིམ་ལ། །མོས་གུས་གསོལ་དེ་བཏབ་དེ་ལས་འོད་འཕྲོས་ནས། །རང་ཐིམ་བྱིང་བའི་རྒྱུ་རྣམས་སེངས་ཀྱིས་དག །བླ་མ་འོད་ཞུ་རང་ལ་ཐིམ་པ་ཡིས། །རང་ལུས་འོད་ཀྱི་གོང་བུ་ཞིང་ཁམས་ཀུན། །སྣང་བར་བྱེད་པ་དེ་ཉིད་ནམ་མཁར་དེངས། །རིག་པ་ངར་དང་བཅས་ཏེ་ཡེ་རེར་ཞོག །རྒོད་ན་བླ་མ་རྡོར་སེམས་སྐུ་མདོག་སྔོ། །པད་འདབ་བཞི་ཡི་རྣམ་པ་ཅན་གྱི་སྙིང་། །དབུས་སུ་བསྒོམ་ལ་འདབ་བཞིར་རྣམ་སྣང་སོགས། །སྐུ་མདོག་དེ་དང་མཚུངས་ལ་རང་རང་གི །རིགས་ཀྱི་དཔའ་བོ་ཌཱ་ཀི་སོགས་ཀྱིས་བསྐོར། །དེ་རྣམས་ཐུགས་ལས་འོད་ཟེར་སྔོན་པོ་འཕྲོས། །བླ་མར་ཐུག་པས་ཕྱོགས

b) Compassion arising as an enemy

Having obtained some degree of joy in meditation, we think, "I must liberate those beings who lack this joy." We abandon meditation, and with many tangible efforts, we accomplish positive compounded actions and cling to them as real. This is called compassion arising as an enemy. Abandoning this attitude, we try, without departing from the compassion which has arisen, to keep our realization stainless.

c) Cause arising as an enemy of the result

We think that to see the profound nature of the mind, we must be learned in all domains. Therefore, we apply ourselves to grammar, debate, and so on, and we abandon the practice of mental calming and superior vision. If we do this, it is what is called the causes [studies] arising as enemy of the result [Mahamudra]. This is not authentic. Meditating with one-pointedness on the profound meaning, we obtain an immaculate knowledge that is not obscured by phenomena of the cycle of manifestation or nirvana.

II. DISPELLING HINDRANCES

1. Illness

Practicing mental calming dispels illnesses of wind. The illnesses of phlegm and bile are eliminated by practicing superior vision. Hot and cold illnesses are both gradually eliminated by mental calming and superior vision. Furthermore, we examine the essence of all illnesses, their form, origin, location, and disappearance. Visualization of sending and taking is emphasized. Illness being unborn, it is the Absolute Body *(dharmakaya)*; being without location, it is the Body of Enjoyment *(sambhogakaya)*; being without cessation, it is the Body of Emanation *(nirmanakaya)*; its nature being emptiness, it is the Body of Essence Itself *(svabhavikakaya)*. Integrating illness to practice as the play of the four Bodies, we see our own mind.

2. Demons [malignant forces]

In the same way, we dispel the hindrances of demons. What appears as a demon is an effect of the magic display of the mind. Looking at the mind as being itself the four Bodies, we eliminate demons in the same way through integrating the four Bodies as the path.

3. Meditation

We have seen the general methods for dispelling the defects of torpor and agitation. Here, they are dispelled through guru yoga. When we sink in torpor, we visualize Lama Amitabha above our head; once the lamas of the lineage melt into Amitabha, we pray to the lama with devotion. Light then radiates from him and melts into us, thoroughly purifying the causes of torpor. Lama Amitabha melts into light and merges with us.

མཚམས་ཐམས་ཅད་དུ། །འོད་ཟེར་གྱིས་ནི་བཀྲུངས་པར་གསལ་བཏབ་སྟེ། །ཕྱག་ཆེན་དང་དུ་མཉམ་པར་བཞག་པས་སེལ། །གཞན་ཡང་བྱིང་རྒོད་གང་བྱུང་དེའི་ངོ་བོར། །མ་ཡེངས་མི་སྒོམ་བཟོ་མེད་ལྷུག་པར་ཞོག གསུམ་པ་ལམ་བགྲོད་ཚུལ་ནི། རྣལ་འབྱོར་བཞིའི་ཚུལ་གྱིས་ལམ་གོང་ནས་གོང་དུ་བགྲོད་ཚུལ་བསྟན་ཅིང་། དེ་རེ་རེ་ལའང་ཆུང་འབྲིང་ཆེ་གསུམ་དུ་དབྱེ་བས་བཅུ་གཉིས་སུ་འགྱུར་རོ། དེ་ལས་དང་པོ་རྩེ་གཅིག་ནི།

།ཐོག་མར་རྩེ་གཅིག་རྣལ་འབྱོར་ཞེས་བྱ་ནི། །སེམས་ཀྱི་རང་ངོ་ཚུལ་བཞིན་ཤེས་པ་སྟེ། །གསལ་སྟོང་མ་འགགས་མཁའ་ལྟར་མཐའ་དབུས་མེད། དེ་ཡི་ངང་དུ་སིང་ངེ་ཡེ་རེ་གནས། །དེ་ལ་ཆུང་འབྲིང་ཆེ་གསུམ་དབྱེ་བ་ལས། །ཆུང་དུ་བདེ་གསལ་ངོ་བོ་མཐོང་བ་དང་། །འབྲིང་པོ་ཉིད་དེ་འཛིན་ལ་རང་དབང་ཐོབ། །ཆེན་པོ་དེ་ཡི་ཉམས་ནི་འཁོར་ཡུག་སོང་། གཉིས་པ་སྤྲོས་བྲལ་ནི།

།སེམས་ཉིད་རྩ་བྲལ་རྟོགས་པ་སྤྲོས་བྲལ་ཏེ། །གཟུང་འཛིན་ཆོས་ཀུན་སྐྱེ་འགག་གནས་གསུམ་དང་། །མཚན་མར་འཛིན་པའི་སྤྲོས་པ་ལས་གྲོལ་ནས། །སྐྱེ་མེད་སྟོང་པ་ཉིད་དུ་སྒྲོ་འདོགས་ཆོད། །དེ་ཡི་ཆུང་དུ་རང་སེམས་སྐྱེ་མེད་རྟོགས། །འབྲིང་པོ་སྣང་འཛིན་སྟོང་འཛིན་གཞི་རྩ་བྲལ། །ཆེན་པོ་ཆོས་ཀུན་སྤྲོས་པའི་སྒྲོ་འདོགས་ཆོད། གསུམ་པ་རོ་གཅིག་ནི། །སྣང་སེམས་འདྲེས་པ་རོ་གཅིག་རྣལ་འབྱོར་ཏེ། །སྣང་སྲིད་འཁོར་འདས་ཆོས་ལ་སྐྱེ་འགག་གི། །སྤྲོས་པ་བྲལ་དང་མ་བྲལ་སྟོང་མི་སྟོང་། །དགག་སྒྲུབ་སྤང་བླང་མེད་པར་གཉུག་མའི་དང་། །མཉམ་པ་ཉིད་གྱུར་དེ་ཡི་ཆུང་དུ་ནི། །གཉིས་བསྡུས་ཆོས་རྣམས་གཅིག་ཏུ་རོ་མཉམ་འདྲེས། །འབྲིང་པོ་སྣང་སེམས་ཆུ་ལ་ཆུ་བཞག་བཞིན། །ཆེན་པོ་ཆོས་ཀུན་མཉམ་ཉིད་དང་དུ་ཞི། བཞི་པ་སྒོམ་མེད་ནི།

།སྤང་གྱི་ཉམས་དང་སྦྱོང་བ་དག་པའམ། །བློ་ནི་གཏན་ཟད་སོང་བར་སྒོམ་མེད་ཡིན། །དེ་ལ་ཆུང་དུ་འབྲིང་དང་ཆེ་གསུམ་ལས། །ཆུང་དུ་བསྒོམ་བྱ་སྒོམ་བྱེད་ཀུན་དང་བྲལ། །འབྲིང་པོ་ལྷུན་གྱིས་གྲུབ་པའི་རང་ས་ཟིན། །ཆེན་པོ་འོད་གསལ་མ་བུ་འདྲེས་པ་ལས། །ཆོས་དབྱིངས་ཡེ

Our body, now a mass of light, illuminates all the realms of manifestation then dissolves in space. We keep this awareness vivid and intense. If we are agitated, we visualize Lama Vajrasattva, blue-green in color, on a four-petalled lotus in our heart. On these four petals, there are Vairocana and the other Conquerors, surrounded by their particular families of dakas and dakinis with the same respective colors. Blue light emanates from their hearts and penetrates the lama. We visualize that all beams of light extend to all cardinal points and intermediate directions. Remaining stable in the state of Mahamudra, we dispel agitation. In addition, whenever torpor or agitation arises, let us remain relaxed in their essence, with nondistraction, nonmeditation, and nonfabrication.

III. TREADING THE PATH

How the path unfolds is shown within the framework of the four yogas. Dividing each of them in three levels—lesser, intermediate, and superior— they become 12 stages.

1. One-pointedness

First, there is the yoga of one-pointedness. Properly knowing the face of the mind, the meditator dwells vividly and intensely in the state of clarity, emptiness, and unimpededness—like space without limit or center. Among the three levels—lesser, intermediate, and superior— in the lesser level, we see the essence of joy-clarity; in the intermediate level, we master meditative concentration *(samadhi);* in the superior level, the experience of meditative concentration *(samadhi)* becomes unlimited.

2. Nonfabrication

Nonfabrication is the realization of the mind in itself and without foundation. When we are free of fabrications—such as the notions of object and subject, the notions of origin, cessation, and location of all phenomena as well as clinging to characteristics—all speculations are eliminated in unborn emptiness. At the lesser level, we realize our own mind as unborn. At the intermediate level, we have no clinging to appearances and emptiness. At the superior level, speculations on fabrication of all phenomena are eliminated.

3. One-taste

The yoga of one-taste blends appearances and mind. Regarding all phenomena of the cycle of appearances and nirvana as equal, we dwell in a natural state. This state is neither devoid nor nondevoid of fabrications such as origin and cessation, emptiness and nonemptiness. It is without action of negating or making exist, and abandoning or undertaking. At the lesser level, paired phenomena are blended into one-taste. At the intermediate level, appearances and mind are like water poured into water. At the superior level, all phenomena are pacified in a state of equality.

ཞེས་ཀློང་དུ་འབྲུམས་གྱུར་ཏོ། །དོན་གཉིས་མཐར་ཕྱིན་རྫོགས་སངས་རྒྱས་པའོ། རྣལ་འབྱོར་བཞི་གསུམ་བཅུ་གཉིས་པོ་དེ་ལམ་དང་སྦྱར་ན། །རྣལ་འབྱོར་བཅུ་གཉིས་པོ་རྣམས་ཕར་ཕྱིན་གྱི། །ས་དང་ལམ་ལ་གལ་ཏེ་སྦྱར་འདོད་ན། །རྩེ་གཅིག་ཆུང་ངུ་ཚོགས་ཀྱི་ལམ་དང་ནི། །འབྲིང་པོ་སྦྱོར་ལམ་དྲོད་རྩེ་ཆེན་པོ་ནི། །བཟོད་པ་ཆོས་མཆོག་ལ་སྦྱར་སྤྲོས་བྲལ་གྱི། །ཆུང་ངུ་མཐོང་བའི་ལམ་དང་ས་དང་པོ། །འབྲིང་པོ་ས་གཉིས་པ་ནས་ལྔ་པའི་བར། །ཆེན་པོའི་སྐབས་སུ་ས་ནི་དྲུག་པ་ཐོབ། །རོ་གཅིག་ཆུང་ངུ་རྟོགས་པས་ས་བདུན་པ། །འབྲིང་པོ་ས་བརྒྱད་ཆེན་པོ་ས་དགུར་སྦྱར། །སྒོམ་མེད་ཆུང་ངུ་ས་བཅུ་ལ་སྦྱར་ཞིང་། །འབྲིང་པོ་རྒྱུན་མཐའི་ས་དང་ཆེན་པོ་ནི། །མཐར་ཕྱིན་ལམ་དང་བཅུ་གཅིག་ས་ལ་སྦྱར། བཞི་པ་འབྲས་བུ་མངོན་དུ་བྱེད་ཚུལ་ནི། །དེ་ལྟར་རྣལ་འབྱོར་བཅུ་གཉིས་རིམ་བཞིན་དུ། །རྒྱུད་ལ་སྐྱེས་ཏེ་སྒོམ་མེད་མཐར་ཕྱིན་པས། །སྒྲིབ་གཉིས་བག་ཆགས་མ་ལུས་ཕྱིར་གཞིལ་ཅིང་། །མཁྱེན་གཉིས་ཡེ་ཤེས་ཡང་ཚོ་ཀུན་རྫོགས་ནས། །རང་དོན་ཆོས་ཀྱི་སྐུ་ལས་མ་གཡོས་ཀྱང་། །གཞན་དོན་གཟུགས་སྐུས་འཁོར་བ་མ་སྟོངས་བར། །རྣམ་རྟོག་འབད་རྩོལ་སྤྲོས་པ་མི་མངའ་བཞིན། །འགྲོ་དོན་མཛད་ལ་ཕྱིན་ལས་རྟག་པ་དང་། །ཁྱབ་པའི་བདག་ཉིད་ལྷུན་གྱིས་གྲུབ་པའོ།། འཇུག་སྨོན་ཚིག་དང་སྦྱར་བྱང་། སླར་སྨྲས་པ། །འདིར་འབད་དགེ་བའི་དངོས་པོ་ཡིས། །སྐྱེ་དང་ཚེ་རབ་དུས་རྟག་ཏུ། །སྲིད་ལས་ངེས་འབྱུང་ཚུལ་གནས་ཤིང་། །བསླབ་གཞི་ཕྲ་མོ་འང་མི་འགལ་ཤོག །གཞན་ཕན་བྱང་ཆུབ་སེམས་མཆོག་གཉིས། །རྨི་ལམ་དུ་ཡང་མི་བརྗེད་ཅིང་། །བསྡུ་དངོས་བཞི་དང་ཕྱིན་དྲུག་གིས། །འགྲོ་ཀུན་བདེ་ལ་འགོད་ནུས་ཤོག །ཡང་དག་དགེ་བའི་བཤེས་གཉེན་རྣམས། །སྲོག་ལྟར་གཅེས་པར་འཛིན་འགྱུར་ལ། །མཉེས་པ་ཀུན་གྱིས་རབ་མཉེས་ནས། །དད་དང་དམ་ཚིག་ལ་གནས་ཤོག །དེ་ཡི་མཐུ་ལ་བརྟེན་ནས་ནི། །སོ་ཐར་བྱང་ཆུབ་སེམས་དཔའ་དང་། །རིག་འཛིན་སྔགས་ཀྱི་སྡེ་སྣོད་ཀུན།

4. NONMEDITATION

Former experiences and feelings are cleansed. It also said that the intellect is entirely exhausted. This is nonmeditation. Of the three levels—lesser, intermediate, and superior—at the lesser level, we are completely devoid of the notions of meditation and meditator; at the intermediate level, we reach spontaneous presence. At the superior level, the mother and daughter clear lights are blended. From then on, we are open to the immensity of primordial awareness of suchness *(dharmadhatu)*. Consequently, the two benefits are fulfilled—Buddhahood is attained.

• *Correspondence between the 12 levels of the yogas (4 x 3) and the paths*

Establishing a correspondence between the fulfilled levels of the 12 yogas and the paths, we arrive at:

- one-pointedness, lesser level = path of accumulation
- one-pointedness, intermediate = path of junction, heat, and peak
- one-pointedness, superior = patience and sublime Dharma
- nonfabrication, lesser = path of vision and first Bodhisattva ground
- nonfabrication, intermediate = from the second to the fifth ground
- nonfabrication, superior = attainment of the sixth ground
- one-taste, realization of the lesser = seventh ground
- one-taste, intermediate = eighth ground
- one-taste, superior = ninth ground
- nonmeditation, lesser = tenth ground
- nonmeditation, intermediate = ground of the end of continuity
- nonmeditation, superior = completion of the path, eleventh ground

IV. ACTUALIZING THE RESULT

In this way, by the 12 yogas born in the stream of mind, we finally reach the nonmeditation. The two veils and latent conditioning are eliminated; the two knowledges, wisdoms, and ripenings are fulfilled. Although not leaving the Absolute Body (*dharmakaya*) which benefits ourselves, through the Formal Body (*rupakaya*) we accomplish the benefit of others, free of concept, effort, and fabrication until samsara is emptied. It is a constant activity and spontaneous omnipresent essence.

།རང་དོན་ཐོས་དང་བསམ་སྒོམ་གསུམ། །གཞན་དོན་འཆད་དང་རྩོད་རྩོམ་གསུམ། །གཉིས་དོན་མཁས་དང་བཙུན་བཟང་གསུམ། །བསྟན་དོན་འཛིན་དང་སྐྱོང་སྤེལ་གསུམ། །དེ་ཀུན་མཐར་ཕྱིན་པར་ཤོག །ངེས་དོན་ཕྱིར་མི་ལྡོག་པའི་གཞུང་། །ཁྱད་པར་གནས་ལུགས་ཕྱག་རྒྱ་ཆེ། །ཚུལ་བཞིན་རྟོགས་ཏེ་གཞན་ལ་ཡང་། །སྤེལ་བའི་བྱེད་པོ་ཉིད་གྱུར་ཅིག །མདོར་ན་ནམ་མཁའི་མཐས་གཏུགས་པའི། །ལུས་ཅན་མ་ལུས་བདག་གོ་ནས། །ཡང་དག་རྫོགས་པའི་སངས་རྒྱས་ཀྱི། །གོ་འཕང་མཆོག་ལ་འགོད་ནུས་ཤོག །མཆོག་གསུམ་རྒྱལ་བའི་བྱིན་རླབས་དང་། །ལྷག་བསམ་རྣམ་པར་དག་པའི་སྟོབས། །སྟོང་དང་རྟེན་འབྱུང་ཟབ་མོའི་མཐུས། །སྨོན་པ་ཇི་བཞིན་འགྲུབ་གྱུར་ཅིག

ཅེས་པ་འདི་ནི་རྗེ་ཞྭ་དམར་དྲུག་པ་ཆོས་ཀྱི་དབང་ཕྱུག་གིས་ཆོས་དྲུག་བདུད་རྩི་ཉིང་ཁུའི་ཁྲིད་ཡིག་གི་སྙིང་པོ་རྩ་ཚིག་སྒོམ་དོན་ཚིགས་བཅད་དུ་བསྡུས་པར་མཛད་པ་ཉམས་ལེན་སྐབས་སྨོན་འདོན་ཤིན་ཏུ་སྟབས་བདེ་བས་ཕྱག་ཆེན་ལ་འདང་དེ་ལྟ་བུ་ཞིག་བྱུང་ན་སྙམ་པའི་འདུན་པ་སྔར་ནས་ཡོད་མུས་ཐོག ད་ལམ་གནས་མདོ་སྐྱ་ཚང་མཆོག་སྤྲུལ་རིན་པོ་ཆེ་དང་དེ་ལ་ཡག་བླ་མ་ཚེ་མཐར་གཉིས་ནས་ལོ་གསུམ་སྒྲུབ་པར་བཞུགས་པའི་སྐབས་གོང་གསལ་ཆོས་དྲུག་རྩ་ཚིག་དེ་ཉིད་ཟུར་དུ་པར་འདེབས་གནང་སྐབས་དེ་དང་ཆབས་ཅིག་ཕྱག་ཆེན་ལ་འདང་འདི་ལྟར་དགོས་ཞེས་དོན་གཉེར་ཅན་འགགས་བསྐུལ་ངོར། ཉམས་ལེན་གསར་བུ་བ་རྣམས་ལ་ཅུང་ཟད་ཕན་དུ་རེ་བའི་ལྷག་པའི་བསམ་པ་བཟང་པོས་ཉེ་བར་མཚམས་སྦྱར་ཏེ། རྒྱལ་བའི་དབང་པོ་དཔལ་ཀརྨ་པའི་གདན་ས་ཆེན་པོ་འོག་མིན་བ་ཤད་སྒྲུབ་ཆོས་འཁོར་གླིང་གི་སྒྲུབ་སྡེ་ཆེན་པོ་ཡིད་འོང་བསམ་གཏན་གླིང་གི་སྒྲུབ་དཔོན་བླ་མའི་མིང་འཛིན་འབོ་དཀར་སྤྲུལ་སྐུ་ཀརྨ་ངེས་དོན་ཆོས་ཀྱི་བློ་གྲོས་ཀྱིས་རྫོར་གླིང་ མི་རིགས་ཞེས་པ་སྨན་ལྗོངས་ཞི་བའི་བསྟི་གནས་འབོ་དཀར་ངེས་དོན་ཆོས་འཁོར་གླིང་དུ་ཕྱི་ལོ་ ༡༩༨༩ ཕྱི་ཟླ་ ༡༢ པའི་ཚེས་ ༡༣ ཤིང་བྱི་ཟླ་ ༡༠ པའི་ཚེས་ ༢༠ ཕུར་རྒྱལ་མེ་རླུང་འགྲུབ་སྦྱོར་དང་ལྡན་པའི་དུས་ཚེས་ཉིན་བྲིས་པ་དགེ་ལེགས་འཕེལ།། །།

By the substantial efforts and virtuous activity in all my births and lives, may I remain disengaged from the activity of becoming and may I not transgress even the slightest fundamental aspect of training (in ethics) in all times.
May I not forget, even in dreams, the two sublime Bodhicittas that benefit others; may I be able to establish all beings in happiness by the four foundations of gathering and the six paramitas.
Regarding the perfectly pure spiritual friends with as much love as for my own life, may I satisfy them with all satisfactions and remain with faith and vows [samaya].
By the power of such wishes, through studying, reflecting, and meditating on all the baskets—those of individual liberation, of bodhisattvas, and of the mantras of the vidhyadharas—may I benefit myself. May I benefit others through explanation, debate, and composition. May I accomplish both benefits through erudition, observance, and good nature. May I accomplish the benefit of the doctrine as its holder, protector, and propagator.
May I realize the changeless philosophy of certainty and, in particular, the Mahamudra of the mode of being [nature of the mind]; may I contribute to the flourishing of the Dharma for others.
In short, may I alone be able to establish all the incarnate beings who inhabit the ends of space, into the sublime state of pure and perfect Awakening.
By the blessing of the Three Jewels and the Conquerors, by the power of perfectly pure great aspiration and by the force of emptiness and profound interdependence, may these wishes be fulfilled.

The Sixth Sharmapa, Choky Wangchuk, wrote a guide for the *Six Dharmas* of Naropa, titled *The Condensed Ambrosia of the Six Dharmas*. I summarized the essence of this text in the form of a root text in verses to recite during the practice. Because while practicing, such a text is very helpful, I thought for some time that we should have one for Mahamudra. Nedo Kuchung Choktrul Rinpoche and Lama Tsethar from Tilyal had wanted, during their three-year retreat, to print the root text of these *Six Dharmas* of Naropa. They then encouraged me to write a similar text for Mahamudra. I conceived of this project for beginners in the practice, with the excellent aspiration to bring them help. This text was written by Bokar Tulku Karma Ngedon Choky Lodro, the lama, master of retreat of the great retreat center of Yi-ong Samten Ling, attached to the seat of the Lord of the Conquerors, the glorious Karmapa, the seat called Omin Shedrup Chokhor Ling. Written in Mirik, district of Darjeeling, a land which is a balm for the mind, at Bokar Ngedon Chokhor Ling, on December 13, 1984, the twentieth day of the 10th month of the wood-rat year, at the moment of the conjunction of Thursday, the eighth constellation, fire, and air.
May virtue increase!

BRIEF GLOSSARY

ACT: Physical action as well as words or thoughts.
NEGATIVE ACT: All negative deeds that deliberately cause others to suffer, and leave an imprint of more suffering on our mind that will condition our experience and vision of the world. *POSITIVE ACT:* Following the law of karma, an act is positive when it creates happiness in us. *TEN NEGATIVE ACTS:* Killing, stealing, sexual misconduct, lying, creating discord, using harsh words, meaningless talking, envy, ill will, and wrong views. *TEN POSITIVE ACTS:* Protecting life, giving, having an ethical conduct, talking truthfully, reconciling people, talking with gentleness, talking about meaningful things, being content, benefitting other beings, and giving up wrong views.

AMITABHA: Buddha of Infinite Light; Buddha of the Lotus Family; manifestation of discriminating wisdom that purifies desire-attachment; associated with the West; red in color.

AWAKENING: State of Buddhahood.

AWAKENING MIND: See *bodhicitta.*

BEINGS: There are six classes of beings: gods, demigods, human beings, animals, hungry ghosts and hell beings.

BODHICITTA: Aspiration to obtain Awakening in order to help all beings. *ABSOLUTE BODHICITTA* is the realization of emptiness of all phenomena. *RELATIVE BODHICITTA* refers to the practice of compassion and is divided in aspiration (limitless love, compassion, joy, and equanimity) and application (practice of the six perfections or paramitas).

BODHISATTVA: Being who follows the bodhicitta path and seeks to obtain Awakening not only for oneself but for the sake of all beings. An ordinary being who commits to practice bodhicitta. One who has attained Awakening and dwells in one of the ten grounds or stages of the bodhisattvas. A bodhisattva can be physically present in our world or abide in domains of more subtle manifestation.

BODHISATTVA POSTURE: Seated with legs crossed, left heel against the perineum, right foot and leg are bent flat in front.

BODY: Ordinary physical body. State of possessing numerous qualities, in Sanskrit, kaya.

BRAHMA ORIFICE: Point situated on the top of the head.

BUDDHA NATURE: Potential of Awakening inherent in all beings.

BUDDHA: One who has awakened. A person, as the historical Buddha Sakyamuni. In Tibetan, *Sangyay. Sang* means purified from the conflicting emotions, duality and ignorance; *gyay* means that the infinite potential of qualities of a being is awakened. *MALE BUDDHAS:* There are five Buddha Families corresponding to the manifestation of five wisdoms, the purification of five poisons, a direction, and a color. *FEMALE BUDDHAS:* They represent wisdom and emptiness as well as the essence of the five elements.

BUDDHAHOOD: Awakened state characterized by wisdom (as knowledge of the true nature of phenomena and their manifestation in the three times), compassion for every being and power to help all beings.
CLARITY: With emptiness, one of the aspect of the nature of the mind. Clarity designates the dynamic aspect which includes the faculty of knowing and creating all manifestation.
CONFLICTING EMOTIONS: Desire-attachment, hatred-aversion, ignorance or mental dullness, jealousy, pride, and so on.
CONSCIOUSNESS: From a dualistic point of view, each object of the senses corresponds to a consciousness. There are six or eight consciousnesses depending on their classification. First, let us consider six consciousnesses:
- visual consciousness (forms)
- auditory consciousness (sounds)
- olfactory consciousness (smells)
- gustatory consciousness (tastes)
- tactile consciousness (tangible objects)
- mental consciousness (imaginary objects)

One can add two other consciousnesses:
- disturbed consciousness or ego consciousness, which corresponds to the influence of conflicting emotions on our relationship to phenomena,
- potential of consciousness or "all-ground consciousness"(Sanskrit, *alayavijnana*), which contains all the latent conditionings of karma.

DAKA/DAKINI: Celestial being liberated from samsara accomplishing awakened activity.
DHARMA: Buddha's teachings or the spiritual path.
DHARMAKAYA: Absolute Body, designating a state beyond any spatial or temporal determination; corresponds to emptiness.
DHARMADHATU: In this case, *dharma* means phenomenon and *dhatu* space. Emptiness as space where appear all manifestations.
DHARMATA: Nature of the mind and phenomena.
EIGHT FREEDOMS: In order to have the precious human existence, one must be free of 1) being in hell, 2) being a hungry ghost, 3) being an animal, 4) being a god, 5) having wrong views, 6) believing in philosophical systems contradicting the Dharma, 7) being born in ages without spiritual teachings, and 8) having physical disabilities hindering the practice of the Dharma.
FIVE AGGREGATES: Physical and mental constituents of a being prisoner of duality and illusion:
- aggregate of forms (physical elements and particularly the body)
- aggregate of sensations (pleasant, unpleasant, or neutral)
- aggregate of perceptions (understanding of the nature of that which produces pleasant, unpleasant, or neutral sensations)
- aggregate of volition (reactions toward perceived objects)

- aggregate of consciousnesses

At a pure level, these aggregates become the nature of the five male Buddhas.

FIVE ELEMENTS: Earth, water, fire, air, and space. They are the symbols of different states of matter. Space designates the emptiness in which all manifestations appear. The essence of the five elements corresponds to the nature of the five female Buddhas.

FIVE POISONS: Desire, anger, ignorance, pride, and jealousy.

FIVE WISDOMS: They are a way of describing the functioning of the awakened mind: discriminating wisdom, wisdom of equanimity, accomplishing wisdom, wisdom of the dharmadhatu, and mirror-like wisdom.

FOUR BODIES: See Dharmakaya, Sambhogakaya, Nirmanakaya, and Svabhavikakaya.

FOUR ENDS: End of birth is death; end of meeting is parting; end of accumulation is exhaustion; and end of building is destruction.

FOUR STRENGTHS: Force of the support (vows and visualization), force of regret, force of the antidote, and force of reject.

FOUR SYSTEMS OF PERCEPTION OF THE FORMLESS REALM: The four unawakened ways of dwelling on thoughts are: limitless space, limitless individual consciousness, nothing whatsoever, and neither discrimination nor nondiscrimination.

GURU YOGA: Practice of prayer and meditation in order to unite our mind with the mind of an Awakened teacher.

KAGYUPA: One of the four great schools of Tibetan Buddhism. The other ones are Gelugpa, Nyingma, and Sakya schools. The Kagyu lineage originates with Marpa the Translator in the 11th century.

KARMA: The law of karma describes the process of cause and effect. It is a three-phase process:

- an *act* leaves an imprint in the mind of the one who acts (cause)
- this *act* is stored in the potential of consciousness and is slowly ripening
- this process is actualized in a particular form of suffering or joy (result)

LAMA (Tibetan): *Guru* (Sanskrit). A spiritual teacher. *ROOT LAMA:* Generally, the lama we recognize as "our" teacher, who gives us initiations, instructions to practice, and explanation of the texts. More particularly, the lama who allows us to directly experience the true nature of the mind.

LHAKTHONG (Tibetan): Vipassana (Sanskrit), superior vision, meditation practice as direct experience of the nature of the mind.

MAHAMUDRA: Literally the "great seal," designates the ultimate nature of the mind as well as the method of meditation to achieve it.

MANDALA: Literally "center and surrounding"; the world seen as an organized universe. Designates a deity with its surrounding environment.

MANDALA OFFERING: Practice during which we imagine offering the mandala of the universe to Buddha, Dharma, and Sangha.

MANTRA: Sacred sounds, the repetition of which helps the mind purify itself and develop its potential for Awakening. For example, the mantra of Chenrezig is OM MA NI PAD ME HUNG.
MIND: This term can refer to the ordinary functioning of the mind called "psyche" as well as the absolute, nondual pure essence of the mind beyond any fluctuations.
MODE OF BEING OF THE MIND: Nature of the mind; Buddha nature; Clear light.
MOUNT MERU: Mountain in the center of the universe in Buddhist cosmology.
MUDRA: Hand gesture done during rituals. *MUDRA OF MEDITATION:* right hand resting on the left hand.
NIRMANAKAYA: Body of Emanation; appears as human or other forms to guide ordinary beings.
NIRVANA: Literally extinguished, cessation. Early definitions included liberation from conditioned existence, ignorance, and conflicting emotions. Later definitions were expanded to include the development of great compassion through skillful means.
PURE SUPPORTS: They are used in meditation. Statues representing the Buddha's body; texts expressing the Buddha's speech; *stupas* symbolizing the Buddha's mind.
PURIFICATION: All negative acts done in this life and in the past lives have left imprints in our potential of consciousness. These imprints will ripen, engendering suffering and obstacles to our spiritual practice. Purification will neutralize these imprints in order to avoid or reduce their effects. A qualified teacher might designate specific practice to do in order to purify oneself.
SAMADHI: State of meditative concentration.
SAMBHOGAKAYA: Body of Perfect Experience, it appears to guide beings in the Pure Lands.
SAMSARA: Cycle of conditioned existence in which each being is born and dies. It is characterized by suffering, ignorance, impermanence, and illusion.
SANGHA: Community of Buddhist practitioners. One distinguishes ordinary sangha from the Noble Sangha, which is composed of those who have attained the bodhisattva levels.
SENDING AND TAKING: Bodhicitta practice of development of love and compassion through which one gives one's positive potential and happiness to others and takes their suffering upon oneself.
SHINAY (Tibetan): Shamatha (Sanskrit). Mental calming. Meditation practice that frees the mind from reacting to the play of thoughts. It can be done with or without support.
SIX PARAMITAS: Six perfections practiced on the Mahayana path. They are generosity, ethics, patience, diligence, concentration, and wisdom.
SUFFERING: Generally it is analyzed on three levels:

- suffering of suffering: physical and mental pain experienced by all beings.
- suffering of change: one experiences suffering when happiness ends.
- suffering of conditioned existence is suffering one undergoes because of the deluded nature of samsara. It ends only when one attains Awakening.

SUFFERING OF THE HUMAN REALM: Birth, aging, sickness, death, sorrow, grief, despair, getting things we do not like, losing things we like, not getting what we wish for, and so on.

SUNYATA: Emptiness. Fact that all phenomena are without independent existence although they manifest.

SUPPORT: Any object of concentration, material or mental used by a practitioner in meditation.

SVABHAVIKAKAYA: Body of Essence Itself, unity of the three first Bodies (Dharmakaya, Nirmanakaya, and Sambhogakaya).

TAKING REFUGE: Placing oneself under the protection of the Buddha, Dharma, and Sangha (the Three Jewels). In the Vajrayana, one takes also Refuge in the Three Roots, lamas, yidams, and dharma protectors.

TEN RICHNESSES: These ten conditions of the precious human existence are divided in two groups. *INNER RICHNESSES* are 1) human existence, 2) birth in country where the Dharma is taught, 3) having physical and mental faculties intact, 4) having a livelihood not opposed to the Dharma, 5) having trust in the Three Jewels. *OUTER RICHNESSES* are 1) a Buddha manifests, 2) a Buddha teaches the Dharma, 3) the teaching remains alive, 4) there are followers of the teaching, 5) there are structures favorable to the practice.

THREE JEWELS: The Buddha, the Dharma, and the Sangha.

THREE SPHERES: The samsaric realms of Desire, Form, and Formlessness.

THREE TIMES: The past, present, and future.

TWO ACCUMULATIONS: *1) ACCUMULATION OF MERIT:* Practice of positive acts allowing us to store energy for the progression on the spiritual path. This accumulation of merit can be done through the practice of giving, making offerings, reciting mantras, visualizing deities, and so on. *2) ACCUMULATION OF WISDOM:* Practice of understanding the empty nature of all phenomena.

VAIROCANA: Buddha of the Buddha Family; manifestation of the wisdom of dharmadhatu which purifies ignorance; Center; white in color.

VAIROCANA POSTURE: It is also called seven-point posture: 1) legs in vajra position, 2) hands in meditation *mudra,* 3) straight spine, 4) open shoulders, 5) chin down, 6) eyes gazing in space downward, and 7) relaxed tongue.

VAJRA POSTURE: It is also called "diamond posture." Seated with legs crossed, first, the left foot on the right thigh and the right foot on the left thigh.

VAJRADHARA: (*Dorje Chang,* Tibetan) Deity holding a vajra and a bell, the Buddha revealing the Tantras.
VARJASATTVA: (Sanskrit), (*Dorje Sempa,* Tibetan) deity of the Vajrayana who is the source of purification practices. The practice of Vajrasattva includes a visualization as well as recitation of a mantra.
VAJRAYANA: Path of Buddhism also called "Diamond vehicle," referring to the part of the Buddha's teachings written in texts of an esoteric nature called tantras. It uses recitation of mantras, and visualizations of deities and works with subtle winds or energies.
VEILS: That which obscures our Buddha nature such as ignorance, latent conditioning, dualistic perception, conflicting emotion, karmic veils, and so on. *TWO VEILS:* Conflicting emotions and dualistic perception that veil our Buddha nature.
VISUALIZATION: Creation of a mental image used as a support in a meditation or ritual. These images can be geometrical forms or deities, moving or still. This exercise is not dependent upon visual perception but upon inner faculty of imagining.
WISDOM PROTECTORS: Deities who, having attained liberation, are able to disperse obstacles and to create conditions favorable to the practice of the Dharma.
YIDAM: A personal deity expressing the pure nature of the mind. A deity upon which one meditates after having received an initiation.

Index

Also published by ClearPoint Press

by Bokar Rinpoche

Chenrezig Lord of Love

Principles and Methods of Deity Meditation

In this book, Bokar Rinpoche describes the nature of Chenrezig (Avalokiteshvara), the most popular deity of Tibet. He clearly sets forth the principles and theory of this meditation using a minimum of technical terminology and then gives instructions for the practice. You will find illuminating teachings about:

- Nature of the deity
- Principles of deity meditation
- Instructions for practice, including visualizations
- How to apply the practice to all aspects of your life

Meditation Advice to Beginners

Bokar Rinpoche shows us how meditation can eliminate our suffering and help us generate a positive mental attitude. He offers comprehensive instructions for the practice of shinay (shamata/mental calming), Lhakthong (vipashyana/superior vision), and mahamudra—including step by step exercises to train the mind.

Death and the Art of Dying in Tibetan Buddhism

Buddhism asserts that all beings live beyond the various fluctuations of this life. Using the wisdom available in Tibetan Buddhism, Bokar Rinpoche explains and guides us through the experience of death and beyond. How can we turn our death into a positive experience? How can we accompany those who are leaving before us?

Profound Wisdom of The Heart Sutra and Other Teachings

By Bokar Rinpoche and Khenpo Donyo

A literal translation of The Heart Sutra followed by a detailed commentary. Our biggest problem is that we see reality through the distortions created by our own mind. Bokar Rinpoche offers a thorough explanation in order to open our understanding. Another chapter is consecrated to anger, and Khenpo Donyo teaches on karma.

By Kalu Rinpoche

Excellent Buddhism contains biographical reminiscences on Kalu Rinpoche, inspiring stories on Buddhist practitioners of the past, and reflections on the relationship between Buddhism and the West.

Profound Buddhism Teaches how to deal with emotions from a Hinayana, Mahayana, and Vajrayana point of view. It also includes teachings about the nature of the mind, compassion, emptiness, karma...

Secret Buddhism reveals the essentials of Vajrayana, empowerments, the six yogas of Naropa, a history of the Kagyupa and Shangpa lineages, and offers some explanations on Tibetan medicine.

Notes

Notes